THE
DIVERSITY
CON

Also by Kent Heckenlively

Plague - coauthored with Dr. Judy Mikovits

Inoculated

Plague of Corruption - coauthored with Dr. Judy Mikovits

The Case Againsts Masks - coauthored with Dr. Judy Mikovits

The Case Against Vaccine Mandates

Google Leaks - coauthored with Zach Vorhies

Behind the Mask of Facebook - coauthored with Ryan Hartwig

The Case for Interferon - coauthored with Dr. Joseph Cummins

Ending Plague - coauthored with Dr. Judy
Mikovits and Dr. Francis Ruscetti

A Good Italian Daughter - Novel

This Was CNN - coauthored with Cary Poarch

Presidential Takedown - coauthored with Dr. Paul Alexander

THE
DIVERSITY
CON

THE SECRETS AND LIES
BEHIND THE SHADY DEI INDUSTRY

DAVID JOHNSON &
KENT HECKENLIVELY, JD

BOMBARDIER
BOOKS

Published by Bombardier Books
An Imprint of Post Hill Press
ISBN: 978-1-63758-921-2
ISBN (eBook): 978-1-63758-922-9

The Diversity Con:
The Secrets and Lies Behind the Shady DEI Industry
© 2023 by David Johnson and Kent Heckenlively
All Rights Reserved

Cover Design by Cody Corcoran

Post Hill Press
New York • Nashville
posthillpress.com

Published in the United States of America

TABLE OF CONTENTS

FOREWORD

by Dennis Prager

For my bar mitzvah I was given a book about great Jewish athletes. Aside from the predictable jokes about it being a short book, padded with large photos and print, I had little interest in it. One would have expected the book to be a home run as a gift for the teenage Dennis Prager. I loved sports and strongly identified as a Jew, having been raised in an Orthodox Jewish home, and attending yeshivas (Orthodox Jewish schools) until the age of nineteen.

But even at the age of thirteen, the idea of having pride in my identity as an Orthodox Jew, struck me as odd. How could I take credit for the good things done by others, simply because they shared my ethnic identity? And what of the bad people—the murderers, thieves, and other societal malcontents—who shared my identity? No group, no matter how large or small, can lay claim to a monopoly on virtue or vice. Maybe it's because I've always marched to the beat of a different drummer, but as a very young man it seemed that every person could only be judged—lauded or condemned—for the things he or she had done.

When I was in college and the slogan "black is beautiful" became popular, I immediately objected to it. How could a race be beautiful? Isn't the idea of a beautiful race, itself a racist idea? It was explained to me that since blacks had been put down for so many years this was a necessary corrective needed to bolster their self-image. It was an entirely understandable explanation, but I recoiled from it. I feared it could metastasize into something dangerous and unexpected, which could harm the very people it was intended to help.

My instinct was correct. "Black is beautiful" soon morphed into "black power," usually accompanied by a raised fist, and the terrifying proclamation that any black who didn't shout the slogan at the top of their lungs must be a "race traitor." And that term really frightened me, as I associated it with Nazi racism, since "Aryans" who helped Jews were labeled "race traitors."

The women's movement followed a similar trajectory, and I came to conclude that race, class, and sex-based group pride was a characteristic of left-wing thought and activism.

Instead of allegiances based on religion, race, or sex/gender, I found my affinity groups were composed of only decent individuals. I was drawn to good people of every race and all classes and both sexes, to people who took responsibility for their lives and understood that their character, not their identity, is what guided their destiny.

This is why I so strongly recommend *The Diversity Con* by David Johnson and Kent Heckenlively, and why it is an honor to write the foreword to the book.

For those who don't know David Johnson, he is the courageous Project Veritas whistleblower who turned over to James O'Keefe the terrifying DEI (Diversity, Equity, and Inclusion) training video he was required to watch as an employee of Hasbro Inc, the multinational giant toy company, which claimed that babies as young as six months old could be racist. Not that it should matter, just as my race shouldn't matter, but David checks all the left's identity boxes: he is a young, black, center-left gay man. Yet he did not recognize the America depicted in the training video as the America in which he had grown up.

I have known David's coauthor, Kent Heckenlively, for many years, having endorsed several of his previous books. In addition, in February of 2023, I interviewed him for his book, *This Was CNN: How Sex, Lies, and Spies Undid the World's Worst News Network*, which he wrote with another Project Veritas whistleblower, Cary Poarch. Kent combines moral clarity and courage with careful and meticulous writing—a rare combination.

During that interview I asked him to comment on the strength of his allegation that the intelligence agencies had infiltrated CNN. He reviewed the history of the CIA infiltrating the media in Operation

Mockingbird, documented by famed Watergate journalist, Carl Bernstein, in a 25,000-word article in *Rolling Stone* magazine from 1977. Additionally, Kent uncovered evidence that twenty-one current high-level individuals at CNN had intelligence experience. This included CNN's National Security Correspondent, Jim Sciutto, who prior to his work at CNN was chief of staff of the U.S. Embassy in Beijing, China from December 2011 to May of 2013, as well as Senior Advisor to Ambassador Gary Locke. In this position, Sciutto would have been privy to our most closely guarded secrets and been required to sign secrecy oaths before receiving any classified information.

All of this was intriguing to me, but it seemed a piece of the puzzle was missing. "Can you tell me that the intelligence agencies are directing CNN's news coverage?" I asked.

Kent didn't hesitate for a second. I recall he said something like, "No, I can't tell you that. What I can tell you is that journalists used to avoid anything which might potentially compromise their objectivity, like having a private dinner with a politician, much less taking government money. It doesn't seem to me that you can be a 'check' on government if you've received paychecks from the government—especially for a position which would give you access to classified documents and requires you to sign secrecy oaths. How does one go back to independent journalism under those conditions? I suspect this is the way the intelligence agencies are continuing Operation Mockingbird because that's the way I would do it. But in answer to your question, no, I cannot prove, nor do I have any evidence that the intelligence agencies are directing the news coverage at CNN."

Reflecting on our on-air discussion during a boisterous lunch at the Cheesecake Factory later that afternoon, with my wife Sue, and my two stepsons, I told Kent his answer was "intellectually honest."

Kent considered my words a great compliment and said that was the standard he always sought. "I think it's important for a writer to tell you what he suspects. But also to make it crystal clear what he has proven, and what he has not."

David and Kent's book is similarly meticulous and intellectually honest. David went undercover for many DEI trainings, cataloguing the propaganda and brainwashing (my term, not necessarily his) techniques of these race and gender hustlers, while Kent's original research details a disturbing pattern of left-wing dark money, emanating mostly from the Tides Foundation, located in San Francisco, CA, to promote racist and Marxist ideas.

You will probably not be surprised to find that the Tides Foundation, and its rivers of leftist dark money are fed by the tributaries of the usual suspects, such as the Bill and Melinda Gates Foundation, various Rockefeller family foundations, and the Google Foundation. And what left-wing enterprise would be complete without the financial support of George Soros and his myriad affiliated groups?

After reading *The Diversity Con*, one remains haunted by a number of questions:

Do these left-wing billionaires genuinely support Marxist ideas? Or are we witnessing the deployment of Marxism as a means of destroying our free-market economy to substitute it with a crony capitalism where entities like Amazon, Google, and others have monopolistic control over society with the protection of the very government agencies that were created to regulate them? Instead of buying from local merchants and contributing to our communities, do they want us cowering behind locked doors, ordering from Amazon and having our meals delivered by Door Dash, and checking our Ring camera to determine if the delivery person who just knocked is friend or foe?

Even more perplexing, why do such people loathe the America that has been so good to them and seek to destroy the freedoms that have characterized the freest and most prosperous society ever created?

Evil men will not tell you their plans, but David Johnson and Kent Heckenlively, through their hard work, may have discovered it.

The best writers raise provocative questions, provide you with critical information, enabling us, their readers, to come to our own conclusions. I have. And those conclusions are, to understate the case, deeply unsettling.

The future of the America you and I so deeply love may depend on whether we confront and discuss the shocking information presented in this book.

INTRODUCTION

WHAT'S THE BIG DEAL?

Diversity, inclusion, equity, anti-racism, Whiteness, acceptance. From the heights of corporate board rooms to kindergarten class rooms, these terms have become common vernacular. "Diversity is our strength" echoes across news platforms, as politicians boast of the ethnic variety of their subordinates.[1] Educators call for increased "equity" in everything from college admissions to math grades in K-12 education, in efforts to prevent minority students from being left behind.[2]

Simultaneously, activists raise alarms about the need for "inclusive" spaces, to prevent troubled LGBTQIA+ youths from taking their own lives in despair. Americans are assured that the conversion into gender-inclusive spaces—whether they're restrooms, full-contact sports, or locker rooms—will only serve to protect the most vulnerable (and bravest) among us. Most critically, youths need access to proper healthcare, a reasonable request.

On their face, none of these requests seem terribly outrageous. In America, we expect that people of any background can rise to the top through merit. We expect our workplaces and schools to advance individuals without preference to race or sex, and generally want as many people as possible to have access to opportunities for advancement. And you would have to be an evil or deeply apathetic person to not want the suicide rate for any demographic to decrease, in particular the rate of young people who have barely experienced the breadth of this world.

With the end goals established, the next issue must be the means with which to reach the intended goal. The path forward must be chosen carefully and verified rigorously, to prevent going in circles or ending up stuck in a worse circumstance than where we began as a society. Furthermore, the people taking the lead must be honest about their intentions, lest our society end up walking into a trap of our own making or the machinations of others.

While America holds lofty ideals of equal opportunity and justice for all, a basic understanding of American history will be enough to know that America has not always lived up to its ideals. Through generations of conflict and reconciliation, from the North Atlantic slave trade through the Civil War and civil rights era, the culture slowly shifted toward individual equality under the law.

In spite of that, racial tensions are reportedly worse today than in previous decades.[3] Protestors blockade streets and highways demanding racial justice in the day, while violent riots in the cover of night leave businesses looted, ransacked, and vandalized, often in the communities of Black or other racial minority groups. From elementary school to college, special-interest groups advocate racially segregated graduations and events, while claiming that nearly half of LGBTQIA+ youth are suicidal.[4]

Even though the stated goal was a society without discrimination, where people from a diverse spectrum of cultures could come together and feel included and exist as equals, we have missed the mark. At some point, we have taken a misstep along the path, having been led astray by false guides. Western society—America in particular—has taken a sharp left turn, and the end point will not be the ideals of the country for which Americans have strived until recently.

The end goal of indoctrinating children with critical race theory (CRT) will be to groom them into becoming advocates of "anti-racism" (the new racial segregation) and allies to the LGBTQIA+ ideology. They will be taught to segregate along race and gender identity, and to "see color" and treat others according to skin color and gender identity, whether real or perceived.[5]

Once they're on the road to being an LGBTQIA+ ally, they may end up railroaded into "gender affirmation," often involving surgery that removes healthy organs, or puberty blockers—drugs that were historically given to sex offenders to medically castrate them.[6] Just as bad, you might enroll your child in a school where the teacher gives them a book on how to masturbate or different sex acts they can perform, under the guise of an "LGBTQIA+ health lesson."

> Blowies: Oral sex is popping another dude's peen in your mouth or, indeed, popping yours in his. There is only one hard and fast rule when it comes to blow jobs—WATCH THE TEETH. Lips and tongue yes; teeth, NO.

> Basically, porn is fine and fun, but it is in no way REAL. You can take ideas, but it's definitely not for beginners. Everyone, including young gay, lesbian, bi, curious, and queer people, is entitled to high-quality, expertly taught sex education.[7]

Children are led directly within the reach of predators who want to exploit and abuse them. This is a situation that all Americans should agree to avoid at all costs. Regardless of political leaning or affiliation, protecting the innocent should be a point of universal agreement. And I do not make these accusations against the CRT advocates and the LGBTQIA+ activists lightly, nor does this come from the perspective of a rightwing, traditional conservative. To state my own biases, I am a center-left libertarian. "I want to smoke weed and open carry at my gay friend's wedding, on the couple's own land, with their home powered by a personal nuclear generator" sums up my personal politics.

Until 2016, I could have been considered a default liberal. I was freshly out of college, not terribly grounded in most of my political positions. I was raised in a Christian household, where we not only went to church on Sunday, but we also volunteered and helped the church to serve the community. While I valued the charity and positive impact on the community, my belief in the faith itself waned in my late teens in favor of philosophy and logic.

At the time, YouTube atheism had become rather popular, which provided a robust challenge to many of the views of my Christian upbringing. Other popular topics of the time were third-wave feminism and gender identity, along with an endless video gallery of angry, emotionally volatile college activists acting under the banner of "social justice."

While their immature outbursts were endlessly amusing, it did pique my curiosity—not only about the subject of their cries but also about the arguments of their opposition. This was my introduction into social commentary, which would develop into an interest in Western politics. For years I watched social commentary from both progressives and conservatives and everything in between, eventually leading up to my attendance at an event in Portland, Oregon. The topic was safe spaces and "bias response teams" featuring Peter Boghossian and Carl Benjamin, where protestors pulled the fire alarm in an unsuccessful attempt to shut down the conversation.[8]

The more I learned about the grievances of these illiberal progressives, third-wave feminists, and social justice warriors, the more I began to truly discover my own values. I valued liberty; the freedom to live and learn as I saw fit so long as I did not harm others' ability to do the same. Unfortunately, the instances of conversation being shut down by progressive activists were becoming more common and widespread as their ideology gained foothold in regular society. As a natural counterforce, conservative voices began to take prominent roles in opposing the advancement of ideological censorship, and while I agreed with some of the arguments, I did not become a conservative myself.

I just wanted to live and learn, free of suppression and free from coercion to bend the knee to ideas I did not support.

This desire came to a crossroads when my employer, Hasbro, hosted a training on implicit bias, racial awareness, and intersectionality for its employees. For the first time in my adult life, I was faced with the choice to stand on my principles or bend the knee and shut up.

Within the first month of my working there, I saw an invitation in my email for a presentation by a group called The Conscious Kid, with the title "Racial Biases and Children." At first, I thought it would be the kind of standard corporate talk that doesn't go anywhere, with diversity, equity, and inclusion sprinkled in as buzzwords.

However, I thought I should record it just in case. I didn't expect it to go anywhere, but within the first two or three minutes, I started to witness what appeared to be overt Marxist propaganda, with claims that within six months of being born, White children exhibit racial biases.

I was shocked that my company was asking me to be a part of something that I deeply morally opposed. More than seventy people were in the meeting, and it didn't seem that anybody was willing to object to the conclusions being drawn. In college I'd become familiar with this ideology, and while living in Portland when radical activists set up the Capitol Hill Organized Protest (CHOP) in Seattle, I'd watched as those who were taken in most fervently by this ideology became more and more racist.

You remember CHOP, it was the area in central Seattle, taken over by extremists, who wanted to defund the police. In the CHOP, they actually had separate areas for White and Black people, claiming racial justice, anti-racism, CRT, and the need to address "structural racism." Of course, the lack of police led to millions of dollars of property damage, and the death of Horace Anderson, a nineteen-year-old Black man.

At the end of the presentation by The Conscious Kid, the presenters specifically asked the engineers to let the lens of "anti-racism" guide and inform the choices we made going forward. They told us that we at Hasbro had a special responsibility, given that as a toy maker we had such direct access to children. I was especially offended, as it was clear that we were supposed to push this ideology on children without the knowledge of their parents.

I'd thought these ideas were crazy when I first became aware of them in Portland, but now it was coming from a major American employer. These progressives were a far cry from the remarkably inclusive blue-collar workers I'd come to know through my previous jobs, even the ones I'd worked with in college. At the end of the meeting, it seemed that only about five of the seventy attendees made any comment, and I couldn't tell whether that silence meant agreement or passive resistance.

I didn't speak up at the time, either, as I was new to the company, but now I had what I thought was an incriminating video. I didn't think that sending it to local news would make a difference, and I didn't trust CNN or Fox News. The only name that came to mind was Project Veritas. I'd seen James O'Keefe, the Project Veritas founder, in a few interviews with people like podcasters Tim Pool and Steven Crowder, and thought that he seemed trustworthy. At the least, he seemed to be an actual journalist and not a propagandist.

I sent the video to Project Veritas through its special email address, which was supposed to keep my identity secret, explaining what I'd seen and recorded. A Project Veritas member messaged me back within a few hours and asked to see the video. We had more discussions, and within a few days Project Veritas set up a meeting with me in Portland.

I realized that if this story was brought to light, I'd likely lose my job. I was consciously aware that this would have an enormous impact on my life. However, I didn't ponder it very long. I tend to think of things as on a weighted scale. On the one side, I could lose my job and possibly be blacklisted from my industry; on the other side, if I didn't do anything, I'd be helping to perpetuate one of the problems in our society about which I complain the most. I was anxious that the actions of organizations like The Conscious Kid were going to increase actual racism in the country.

I figured the worst-case scenario was that I'd go back to working at the blue-collar factory job I'd left a month earlier, but at least I'd have my self-respect. However, much sooner than I expected, I was asked to fly to New York to be interviewed by James O'Keefe for a story that would be released online and at the Turning Point USA conference in July 2021 in Florida. Project Veritas offered to alter my voice and distort my face for the interview, but I thought that would blunt the message of transparency I wanted to get across.

The videotape began with James sitting across from me in the Project Veritas studios, him in a gray suit, while I was wearing a purple dress shirt, gray jacket, and glasses that accent my "nerd" persona. The glasses kept falling down my face, requiring me to push them back up several times during the interview:

> **JAMES O'KEEFE:** Tell me your name and what you do for a living.
>
> **DAVID JOHNSON:** My name is David Johnson. I'm a packaging engineer for Hasbro.
>
> **O'KEEFE:** And why did you decide to come to Project Veritas?
>
> **JOHNSON:** I decided to come to Project Veritas because I oppose the indoctrination of children they wanted to push. And I felt that people needed to know about it.
>
> **O'KEEFE:** And how are they indoctrinating children?
>
> **JOHNSON:** They are attempting to covertly push critical race theory through the branding and messaging of their products.
>
> **O'KEEFE:** (Pointing to a graphic from The Conscious Kid presentation at Hasbro.) Explain what we're looking at here.
>
> **JOHNSON:** This is the program developed by The Conscious Kid, which is working with Hasbro; I'm not sure exactly to what extent. This is their program

to teach children about…racial bias, at an early age, before they're able to understand what race really is, and what racism is.

O'KEEFE: Is this a mandatory, all-hands training?

JOHNSON: Yes. This meeting was attended by at least forty-four people. I remember it being more on my screen. [I recalled it being more than seventy people.] But it was mandatory for me.

O'KEEFE: How much do you know about this non-profit which developed the training on this, The Conscious Kid? What can you tell us about that?

JOHNSON: This was actually the first time I'd heard about them, at this meeting. Following this, I did some research and they're working for a few other very large organizations, like Google, the NFL, Nickelodeon, who is also a big partner with Hasbro.

O'KEEFE: Now, Hasbro isn't their only heavy hitter.

JOHNSON: No.

O'KEEFE: As you mentioned, they work with the NFL Players Association, MGM, Nickelodeon, and YouTube.

JOHNSON: That's like a large share of the markets for children's entertainment. Hasbro is already a huge company because they already have everything from My Little Pony to Transformers. But YouTube is almost the main hub where they go for entertainment, now. If they're using YouTube to push this ideology, that's going to have very far-reaching and huge and wide implications.

O'KEEFE: You sent this tape to us the same day that you recorded it, correct?

JOHNSON: Yes.

O'KEEFE: Why was it so important to you to get this tape to us immediately?

JOHNSON: Originally, it was out of shock. I couldn't really believe what I was hearing and reading. It was just so—and this word is overused—but it was overtly racist, and very, very discriminatory. The first thing I thought is that *I have to tell people about this.* Just because of how big I knew the company is. And this is before I knew The Conscious Kid had other connections. Just that Hasbro itself was massive enough that people need to know this is being pushed on children.

As the conversation continued, James asked a number of other questions, such as if I'd ever blown the whistle on anything before.

The answer?

No.

I told James I'd seen some of his whistleblower videos and had always been impressed by the people who risked everything. When he asked what bothered me the most, I told him it was that The Conscious Kid was assigning blame to an entire group of people based on their skin color, not their actions.

James played a section of the presentation, in which the speaker claimed that by three to six months, babies were already expressing preference along racial lines. Two-year olds allegedly start to exclude other children based on their skin color. Two-year-old racists were an absurd concept to me. From there, the presentation claimed that between ages three and six, White children are beginning to use racist language.

I was astonished that the presenters were claiming that not only were the children racist, but so were their parents simply because they were White. From their view, I belonged to one of the most hated groups in America and should have deeply felt this prejudice throughout my life. I was twenty-six years old, Black, and gay—but I did not grow up with prejudice. That's not the America in which I grew up.

Sorry.

Not my experience.

I was invited to the Turning Points USA conference in Florida to appear on stage with James O'Keefe, and I accepted. Even though I felt comfortable with conservative thought, I still had a sliver of worry that conservatives might not accept me because I was Black, gay, and not conservative politically. James played the tape at the end of his talk as I waited backstage, and when I stepped out on the stage, I got a standing ovation.

I got through my presentation with James, and he mentioned that his group had started a fundraising campaign on my behalf, as Project Veritas didn't expect that Hasbro would continue to employ me. (Hasbro must have had really good lawyers, because they decided that the company would make no public comment about my allegations, simply letting my six-month contract expire, and not rehiring me.) After my appearance with James, I remained at the conference and was amazed by how many people wanted to talk with me and thank me for what I'd done.

My story must have resonated with people because of the sheer number of anguished parents and disgruntled patriotic-minded people who came to tell me about their own stories after. Students who were suspended from class over challenging claims that they were inherently racist or sexist, or other regular people who'd endured their own "diversity" training in their place of work.

People of all backgrounds, skin colors, and creeds coming together to find out what was going wrong in the country they loved. Questions I could not answer at the time and spent the following year learning as much as I could about.

I came to learn of the true horrific aims of the CRT and gender activists though immersing myself in their trainings firsthand and reading the founding texts that spawned these ideologies. Directly from the source, this book is an explanation and demonstration of the methods of Marxist ideology, and the effects that they have on American society.

David Johnson, 9/3/2021

1

TROJAN HORSES MAINTAINED WITH SNAKE OIL

How do you convince people to do something that is against their own best interests? Going up to people and instructing them to drink a bottle labeled "poison" isn't likely to convince anyone. One method could be to disguise the harmful elixir as something neutral, such as water, or perhaps even as something specifically healthy.

Alternatively, over a longer period of time, a campaign of propaganda could change the perception of consuming poison: casting doubt on the actual harm, changing the term from "poison" to "Candy Blue-42," or spreading the idea of the potential benefits of consuming it. This would of course require an enormous amount of money, influence, and resources, something unavailable to the average person. Some of those nine-figure receipts are presented later in this book.

In colleges, many of the top cultural topics began as deconstructive critiques of legal studies, originating with the efforts of figures such as Kimberlé Crenshaw and Derrick Bell in the late 1980s. Crenshaw is credited with creating the term "intersectionality" in her 1989 paper "Demarginalizing the Intersection of Race and Sex: A Black Feminist Critique of Antidiscrimination, Doctrine, Feminist Theory and Antiracist Politics."[9] The original idea behind the paper is:

a Black woman will experience unique and greater levels of oppression in society than either a Black man or a White woman, due to the "intersection" of racism and sexism. Broaden this framework to include race, ethnicity, sex, and gender, and you have the general idea behind intersectionality. The more marginalized identities one can claim to represent, the higher one's degree of perceived oppression and lack of privilege.

The concept was later adopted by Ibram X. Kendi, using intersectionality as a building block for "anti-racism" and going on to become a best-selling author, the founding director of the Antiracist Research and Policy Center at American University in Washington, DC, and columnist for *The Atlantic*.

> *Intersectional Black identities are subjected to what Crenshaw described as the intersection of racism and other forms of bigotry, such as ethnocentrism, colorism, sexism, homophobia, and transphobia. My journey to being an antiracist first recognized the intersectionality of my ethnic racism, and then my bodily racism, and then my cultural racism, and then my color racism, and then my class racism, and, when I entered graduate school, my gender racism and queer racism.*
>
> —*Ibram X. Kendi,* How to Be an Antiracist[10]

This is not how most people experience or are educated about these topics. Is critical race theory (CRT) taught in schools and colleges? Yes, it is, though mostly through indirect means. For those who claim that CRT and queer theory are not taught in grade schools, the argument is usually along the lines that teachers and instructors are not reading the scholarly works of CRT to children because they're college theories, therefore it is not being taught—an incredibly limiting and convenient definition used to gaslight critics.

In truth, CRT is being taught in grade-school classrooms, colleges, and workplace seminars alike. It is taught through praxis—the practical application of a theory. Theory in practice.

The way praxis works is fairly simple: instead of presenting the core teachings of CRT directly as academic literature, the core teachings are presented within other academic fields, as alternative history, or as seemingly neutral corporate policy or training. Through intentionally subversive methods, it becomes easy to indoctrinate those who are unsuspecting, which is why children and young adults make the ideal targets of radical propaganda.

In the summer of 2022, I enrolled in a series of courses to experience these trainings myself. The first seminar I attended was called "Diversity, Equity, and Inclusion: A Beginner's Guide," and the program seemed a good place to start. The beginning of understanding anything starts with understanding the language used, and that was my goal. What do proponents of diversity, equity, and inclusion (DEI) and CRT *actually mean* when they use these terms that are thrown around so often in modern discourse? My instructor informed me that would be the first topic, so I was in the right place.

The first instructor was a young Black man named Ulysses Smith in his early thirties with a bright smile. Wearing slim-fit business casual attire with an eccentric haircut, and a slight effeminate nature to his mannerisms, he began the lecture:

> *Diversity* is an acknowledgment of difference.
>
> Diversity has come to become synonymous with "underrepresented groups," which is an incorrect practice. In this context, diversity translates to "underrepresented minority recruiting" (URM). "Our diverse hires" translates to our "URM hires."
>
> Strong recruiters should automatically be ensuring talent comes from a diverse background, so "diverse" will not mean "our minority hires" but instead "all of our employees come from different backgrounds" (to normalize DEI as common practice).
>
> Diversity alone is an incomplete narrative, focused only on the composition of a group.[11]

A lot of acronyms at the start, but that's pretty standard for corporate America. Nothing very disagreeable so far. Recruiters should look at a wide range and select the best fit for the position, which may result in a diverse workforce. Not entirely certain why "acknowledgement of difference" is automatically a strength. The next section is where I detected a deviation from the values of colorblindness that I had been taught by my parents and in school. Smith continued:

> *Tolerance* suggests there is a limit to how much we are willing to deal with at any given time. It does not elicit the most positive emotion in people.
>
> *Inclusion* means that all people are accepted, respected, meaningfully engaged, and able to participate in the full activities of an organization, regardless of identity.[12]

I've always understood the principle of tolerance to express a "live and let live" philosophy, suggesting that if what you're doing isn't negatively impacting me or others, I might have an opinion but live as you want. However, the problem arises when "inclusion" means that I must live by those principles. The simple fact is that there are people who regularly act in ways I do not accept or respect. Think of bosses who degrade their employees over trivial mistakes, parents who terrorize or harm their children, individuals or organizations which blatantly violate the law and harm the public.

Everyone reserves the right to be intolerant of what they consider to be unacceptable behavior and I will die before I give up that right. On a broader scale, defining what is intolerable is a core aspect of any culture or subculture. If there are behaviors that we consider valuable, constructive, and desired, then behaviors that are destructive, undesirable, and detrimental also exist. The next section defined "belonging" and Smith continued,

> *Belonging* is the feeling that you are a valued and essential part of a team. Meaning, you feel like you are not an "expendable cog in the wheel.[13]

It's a wonderful sentiment and something we'd like to be true, but it just isn't reality in many jobs, and is heavily subjective depending on the person. How can you realistically enforce a feeling, and mandate that others feel a certain way?

As for general advice about life, it's incredibly destructive. Here's the terrible truth about the world: nobody owes you anything—not comfort, not respect.

You do not deserve respect simply because you exist and draw breath upon the face of the earth. You earn respect by the quality of your actions and their impact on others. If at your job you can figure out how to make yourself indispensable by doing things that others find difficult or impossible, you will have gone a long way toward earning the respect of those in your company. Generally speaking, those who demonstrate courage, great talent, wisdom, or humility earn the respect of those around them. They hold respect because of their virtues, not because it was mandated by the HR department.

Now under the category of "Belonging," Smith mentions those things that create a sense of belonging, and in general, I agree. He mentions "pride" and expressing the desire for a company to be a "winning organization," that one's superiors be "respectable, accomplished people," and that the company be "successful and highly performing."

All of that is wonderful, but there is a remarkable lack of agency and self-accountability in those criteria. Even when working a low-skill job, there can be useful experience to be gained, and having pride in one's work is up to the worker, not the company.

The final section under "Belonging" was titled "Fulfillment" and asked, "Is my work fulfilling and enjoyable?" and "Is there meaning in my work?"[14] Again, we run into the issue of trying to create rules based on entirely subjective feelings. The sewer cleaner who works sixty hours a week to provide for his family may find his work fulfilling. Someone with an inflated ego in that same position who yearns to be a multimillionaire may find it humiliating and degrading. There is no universal way to ensure that employees feel fulfilled.

The next section was titled "Exploring Equality and Equity" and it's where the shift away from Martin Luther King, Jr.'s principles became especially pronounced. With a grin on his face, Smith began to explain the problems with equality:

> While *equality* is not bad, research shows that treating everyone the exact same way can have very disparate outcomes. This is because equality does not take background into account. So, allocating the same amount of resources to people may not get everybody to the same outcome.
>
> *Equity*: Individuals are given the resources they need to be their most successful selves. Acknowledges we all begin from different places, aims to ensure we reach the same goals with the appropriate level of resources for each of us.[15]

In order to demonstrate the difference between equality and equity he showed two pictures of three boys at a fence watching what seems to be a professional baseball game. One boy appears to be a teenager, the second seems to be around eight, and the third is a toddler.

In the "equality" picture, all are standing on a single wooden box. The teenager can see perfectly (he's actually towering over the fence), the eight-year-old can see fine, and the toddler cannot see anything.

The "equity" picture has the teenager with no box, since he can see over the fence simply by standing, the eight-year-old is standing on a single box, while the toddler is standing on two boxes. All of them can now watch the game.

But, in order to maintain a meritocratic system, a system where individuals reap the rewards or consequences of their own actions, the system in which they operate must treat them as individuals before all else. In practice, that means not introducing additional barriers to some people. Introducing obstacles to some is typically what we call discrimination.

In the fence example, the toddler cannot see the game until obtaining the box from the teenager. While it's an admiral outcome for all parties to see a baseball game—a treasured American pastime—it does not translate to all situations, especially those with real consequences.

Assuming that equal outcomes are a desirable goal, would it be acceptable to dock the pay of a high-achieving person to equalize him or her with a lower-achieving colleague? If the lower achiever was given a pay boost instead to meet the pay rate of dedicated employees, the high achievers will have no incentive to work hard, much to the detriment of the company's productivity.

Alternatively, if it is known beforehand that one is a diligent worker and the other is lazy, would it be acceptable to give the lazy one less work while the other picks up the slack? Of course not. Nor does this work in colleges and universities, as anyone who has ever dealt with an idle teammate has experienced. Consider that it is not the goal of a college or company to ensure that its students or employees achieve equal outcomes. It is to facilitate education and skill development for individuals, and to encourage them to do their job.

Without explanation, Smith began the next section with these questions:

> Are there groups here that are not being promoted or given development opportunities? What can be done to ensure this group is represented?
>
> In recruiting and hiring: Recognize which groups are underrepresented in the workforce, what practices can be implemented to correct the misrepresentation?[16]

Isn't this line of reasoning making an enormous assumption? *Why* is it that people with certain identities seemingly require systemic assistance in order to achieve equity? It could easily be considered a racist statement to rephrase this mindset as "minority groups need assistance because they're incapable of competing." I studied something practical—packaging engineering—and didn't need any extra advantages. Ironically, I was placed in a terrible position in my first job, not having what I needed, still made it work, and ended up becoming more productive than co-workers with better resources.

Furthermore, the class presentation switched from discussing an equal outcome between individuals to equalizing entire identity groups, vastly compounding the problem. What happens when one identity group has a majority in the hiring pool? Turning away qualified applicants to fill a quota will lower the overall quality of hires if merit has taken a backseat. Only in hypotheticals do two applicants of absolute equal qualifications appear.

My advice to anybody entering the job market is to develop the skills you need so that you are desirable to an employer, or to accumulate enough skills to become reliably self-employed.

>><<

In the next section, Smith attempted to convince us that DEI is the key to financial success. Unfortunately, he didn't understand the concept of cause and effect.

The section was titled "Behavior of Champions," and Smith tried to make the argument that companies that followed DEI practices were likely to be more successful that those that don't:

> The addition of inclusive practices and building diverse teams have a direct impact on an organization's bottom line.

> Research shows diverse teams are more productive, engage in more complex problem solving, and produce better outcomes.

> This is because having different backgrounds and perspectives on a team allows for biases to be checked and lets someone see the world through the lens of someone else.[17]

There's a good deal with which I agree. You need diverse viewpoints to anticipate problems and generate solutions. But this is diversity of viewpoint and experience, not diversity of skin color or gender.

Do you believe I, as a Black man, might have a completely different viewpoint than my White colleague about how to engineer a box? Will my sexuality affect my design work?

I've always found that level of education, individual interests, and work ethic are a better gauge of whether I will agree with or respect another person's opinion or work. It's not an immutable characteristic about you, such as your skin color, gender, or sexual orientation that is important, but the quality of your thinking and your skills. To support the claim that diversity promotes financial success, Smith provide these statistics:

> Companies with racial and ethnic diversity are 35% more likely to have financial returns above their respective national industry medians.

> Companies in the top quartile for gender diversity are 15% more likely to have financial returns above their respective national industry medians.[18]

Let's break that claim down. The McKinsey report quoted above does not give any reason or connection between the increased diversity and the increase in company performance. It could very well be any number of other factors that go into the maintenance of a company. Alternatively, the highest-earning companies may be adopting these policies through participatory governance structures, without regard for impact on their performance.

The more successful a company is, the more likely it would be both to wish to bring about societal change, and in the alternative, the more likely it would be to be looking for the next new thing to bring it a competitive advantage, either in its marketing or recruitment efforts. *Join with us, we're the most forward-looking company in promoting diversity and equity.* Since colleges have become breeding grounds for wokeness, it only makes sense that recruiters would pander to the current dynamic, and often they're trained to do just that.

>«

During the Cultural Revolution in China, those who were declared enemies of the Communist Party were often required to write confessions of their thought crimes.

But when it comes to critical race theory and critical identity theories at large, your crime occurs before you have even had any thought or taken any action. Your crime is inherent in you, based on the privileged identity groups you can claim or to which you can be assigned. By pre-determining which groups have privilege and which do not, the same class-conflict can be fomented.

Smith begins the following segment—innocently called "Navigating Identity"—where he informs us students of our sins.

Smith explains that a prerequisite to being successful in any diversity initiative is to understand the identities that make up a person and how those identities interact with society.

But the segment wasn't about knowing all the things that make you awesome as an individual. It was about all the things that make you a guilty or victimized person as a member of a certain group. According to Smith, we needed to understand that, "You and everyone are a complex web of identities that have an impact and will affect how we interact with the world."[19] He continued to spin out this idea:

> Social identity is a reflection of who you are based on your membership in a given group.
>
> Groups most common to us:
>
> Gender
> Race
> Ethnicity
> Sexual orientation
> Religion

For many people, these identities have a profound impact on their sense of belonging and affinity.

In any situation, identities belong to one of two types:

Agent identities: Groups that hold unearned privileges in society.

Target identities: Identities that are disenfranchised or exploited.

Privilege is a set of special advantages that are made available only to certain groups.[20]

This is about where the mask began to slip from this gilded horse. Although I'll delve into this subject later in greater detail, the formulation of "agent" and "target" identities is classical Marxist/Communist thinking. Just change "agent" and "target" to "bourgeoisie" and "proletariat" and you have a stock Communist dialectic. The ideas being promoted aren't new or progressive; in reality, they're the worst ideas from the twentieth century repackaged for American consumption in the twenty-first century.

In reality, in most workplace situations, it would be more valid to divide the two categories of workers into "competent people who add value to the system" and "those who do not currently possess the skills required to be highly valued by the system."

Smith then gave examples of agent and target identities, using himself as the basis. His agent identity was being a man born in the United States, having privileges because of gender and citizenship, while his target identities are being Black and a member of the LGTBQIA+ community, who suffers because of his race and sexual orientation.

Ironically, I find myself in a similar situation. Am I meant to feel remorse or resentment over my sexuality and skin color? I also find it rather presumptuous to state for a fact that my life is worse off because of my skin color or sexual preferences. The point of being diverse and inclusive was to avoid these prejudicial mindsets, yet we're being taught to embrace them as something good.

Smith moved into discussing the "cycle of socialization," which depicted a process by which we're born into "particular circumstances," then "receive messages about who we are," and these messages are then "reinforced by institutions," a cycle which either leads us to obtaining societal power or receiving societal violence, at which point we can decide whether or not to break the cycle.[21]

It's remarkable to consider that the picture being painted of the world is incredibly bleak, where minorities are born into certain situations and cannot conceive of any way out of them. In the world depicted by the seminar, individuals have little or no power to affect their destiny or improve their lot in life. It also reinforces the class-conflict worldview, as the only way these identities interact is either to reinforce privilege or discrimination.

Just in case you didn't feel that your victim status was fully realized by the first few suggestions, in the next section, Smith helpfully provided a few more categories, such as "social class, age, disability, national origin/citizenship, tribal/indigenous affiliation, body size or type," and finally, of course, "additional."[22]

This interwoven web of identities adds a layer of complexity to an already inconceivable problem. We began discussing the desire to equalize outcomes across race, sex, sexuality, and gender, and then expanded to include categories like body size and disability. Smith did not even prove that these inequities across identity groups are due to discrimination, an assumption the entire lesson was built upon.

In an attempt to address this point, Smith began the following segment, "Unconscious Bias" with an explanation of how a person's decisions are the result of unintentional discrimination:

> *Unconscious bias* is our tendency to make quick judgments and assessments by relying on patterns and stereotypes without realizing it.

> We create narratives about people or entire groups based on the limited information we have about them. This can be detrimental to inclusive environments.

> We often don't think about our agent identities. That's part of having privilege.[23]

The class was then given a test on our implicit biases, examining our association between COVID-19 vaccines and the concept of "harm." I am not certain why this was the example used, but I feel it is worth mentioning that I scored "a slight association between harm and COVID-19 vaccines."

Unconscious bias provides a very convenient cover when lacking proof that unequal results are the result of discrimination. By poisoning the well beforehand, all actions can be presumed to be a result of bias, thus confirming a previously held belief. But relying on patterns and stereotypes is part of what has helped humanity to survive. One cannot say that bias is an inherently unhelpful or inherently wrong tool.

Let's say I'm walking down the street in broad daylight, and I see a young woman pushing a baby stroller. I am not on high alert. In fact, I'm immediately in a good mood. I might stop to say hello, compliment her cute baby, maybe even ask if she's been able to get much sleep. This reaction is a bias as much as it is a social convention. These are the things which unite us in our common humanity. My bias tells me not to expect the woman to pull an AK-47 from her stroller and blow me away.

By the same token, let's say I'm in an urban area, it's late at night, and I see a group of rough-looking Black teens approaching me. Just because I'm also Black doesn't mean they won't rob me. The fact that I speak like most college-educated White people might even put me in *more* danger from a gang—regardless of their race or mine.

One of the things which greatly annoyed me is the version of reality presented by such organizations as The Conscious Kid, lacking the understanding of how humans have related to each other throughout history. Here is Smith's advice on "learning to listen," a critical part of uplifting targeted identities.

Listen: Listen until you hear the principle or core of what is being said. Consider it while abandoning your status and privilege, while recognizing theirs.

Affirm: This is the "unnatural part." Express the connection or common feeling with the person, saying you will not attack, dismiss, or hurt the person.

Respond: Speak openly about your social identity to express your thoughts to others. If you agree with the person, this is the part to affirm that. If not, silence is an acceptable response.[24]

Smith went on to describe a conversation between two male co-workers, with one stating: "I think it would be fine for gay people to have civil unions, I just don't see why they have to call it marriage."

First, we're instructed to listen, as if the person expressing that opinion is being reasonable. Second, as the affirming step, we're to express a platitude to show some support for the person's position, such as "I'm glad you like civil unions. They provided same-sex couples some of the privileges of marriage." For the response, we're to express concerns with the other person's position, such as "My issue is defining marriage between only a man and woman. To me, marriage is a commitment between two people who love each other." And finally, we're to inquire further and propose a solution, such as "Some have suggested we call all state-performed ceremonies civil unions and leave the word marriage for religious ceremonies. How about that?"

While I'm glad the course supports dialogue with people who have different views than one's own, there are a few problems with this method that harm genuine understanding.

While it's important to listen, if you're only listening within the context of status and privilege you will possibly neglect important factors, such as merit and time invested by that individual to reach his current status in life. Beginning with his privilege also introduces assumptions about how his life went because of his race or gender that may not be true for that person.

The second step, finding common ground, is a genuinely good tactic to foster productive dialogue. However, this tactic sometimes does not work if presented with an idea that cannot be compromised on. If someone proposes bringing back segregation, or proposes a lecture to middle schoolers on the scholastic use of sex toys, there is no compromise to be had. Some ideas just need to be rejected outright because of the harm they can bring.

At the "responding step," the problems that stem from listening within the context of "privilege" are immediately apparent. If in agreement with a statement, we are encouraged to respond in affirmation with advancing social identity politics. If not, we are to remain silent. The first problem is: the statement may have nothing to do with social identity. And responding in such a manner may serve to disrupt some productive conversations that are occurring. If the issue is "how to best reduce rates of violent crime in inner cities," knowing how sexuality intersects with society isn't going to be more useful than understanding more direct causes, such as social policies and organized crime.

The second problem: There are situations in which it's acceptable or even necessary to reject the statement instead of affirming it. Ideas that are wrong or misinformed should be challenged; if an idea is well grounded in reality and merit, it will stand on its own. If not, the idea deserves to be discredited and both parties can understand why.

Take the *purely hypothetical example* that someone suggests that "men are capable of giving birth." A pure hypothetical that has become a topic of intense debate among several elected Democrat officials.[25] According to Smith, if I don't agree I should just be silent.

Yet, discouraging someone from speaking his mind just to appease others is essentially form of oppression in my view.

Still, taking the lesson to heart, I kept my mouth shut as Smith moved to the next section: "Attitudes to Actions." He began by stating that being aware of the problems in American culture is not the final step, but the first one. Now that we have begun to view the world in terms of privilege and identity, it's time to build coalitions to actually change the culture. Smith states that the goal is to create structures that promote diversity, while also fostering an inclusive environment in a company. This can be achieved by:

1. Establishing inclusion taskforces to spearhead organizational change.
2. Launching an employee-resource-group program to support advocacy.
3. Create intentional and ongoing educational opportunities across the organization.[26]

Ignoring that none of these actions adds to the productivity of the company, there is a pattern in these strategies. The presenter understands that recruiting and HR act as gateways to the company. If that gateway can be used to filter out some identities in favor of others or can be constructed to promote certain ideas, the entire culture of a company can be shifted over time.

Going into further detail, Smith explains that a successful task force must have a clearly defined purpose, one that justifies the need to focus on DEI. In addition, diverse representatives from across the organization, including leadership positions, should be included in its formation. The reason being: this establishes the widest web from which influence and drive can be used to further impress DEI upon the company. It is especially useful for executive members of the company to be involved. This not only grants credibility to the task force, but also the leverage and influence of an executive.

Finally, a task force should have measurable and actionable goals over a set timeline. Such a goal might entail "raising the proportion of minorities from X to Y by the end of the fiscal year."

It is not only a top-down approach, using the influence of a CEO position, but also a decentralized bottom-up strategy that spreads the objectives of diversity across the entire organization. However, task forces are often met with pushback from employees due to their compulsory nature.

The second strategy presented to the class is the creation of an employee research group (ERG). Unlike task forces, these are voluntary and are typically formed around the interests of a demographic characteristic, such as race, gender, ethnicity, national origin, sexual orientation, or ability status.[27] Unlike social clubs that generally center around a shared interest or skill, ERGs should be designed to serve marginalized demographics: "ERGs are formed specifically to serve as an affinity space for underrepresented or underserved populations. In the United States, these groups are referred to as protected classes," said Smith.[28]

The focus group is created to find and raise awareness of the inequitable identity group representation in the company, and then is tasked to resolve it. Combined with task forces, not only is this group creating a problem where none existed before, it is a self-perpetuating cycle that guides the company into a diverse "Catch 22."

For example, take a task force that has a goal of increasing the proportion of Black employees in leadership from 20 percent to 30 percent by the end of the year, with an ERG formed to promote desired Black inclusivity. If the goal is met through hiring quotas, promotion targets, or other discriminatory action, the following year the target will inevitably be raised once again to achieve "parity" or "equity."

If the target is not met however, the task force can now claim that the company is not doing enough to uplift these legally protected groups, without ever needing to prove that the inequity was the result of discrimination in the first place. This is a lose-lose situation for the company, and a certain victory for advancing diversity and equity policies.

In workplaces, DEI is often disguised as HR training or packaged under trainings that address "systemic" biases or inequities. My first personal experience was during the "Racial Bias in Child Development" training at Hasbro.

It was during this meeting that Hasbro began with the premise that because of the influence on and access that Hasbro has to children and—by extension—to their parents, it was Hasbro's responsibility to disrupt inequity in all its forms:

> Intersectionality is important. Cause when we talk about race, a lot of folks think we're talking about just race. When we talk about race, we talk about it through an intersectional lens. So, we're talking about the ways through which race intersects with gender, intersects with class, intersects with sexual orientation, intersects with faith. All these different aspects that come [together] to make a unique racial experience for all of us.
>
> —Ramon Stevens, founder of The Conscious Kid, at Hasbro Racial Bias in Child Development training[29]

Hasbro employees were taught that children as young as three use racial stereotypes to determine their peer group, with a strong bias in favor of Whites and against Blacks. By age five, White children hold the same level of racial bias as their parents, while, stunningly, minority children do not. And by middle school, White children engage in segregation, and by high school, both Black and White teens are unable to interact with each other—the mere presence of someone outside one's own racial group triggers a flight or fight response. And the only way to prevent such an outcome is to educate these unaware children about "anti-racism" and the intersections of identity and privilege.

Just as Smith had described, I could now see how Hasbro was captured by the lofty-sounding ideals of diversity, inclusion, and equity. As one of the largest childrens' toy and games designers in the world, the company was a golden opportunity to be exploited by activists: knocking on the gate with a smile and a bottle of society-fixing snake oil, promising to solve issues, while fomenting and sowing the seeds of the very discrimination and prejudice they're claiming to resolve.

2

SPINNING A WEB OF RAINBOW YARN

*To be antiracist is to reject not only the hierarchy of races
but of race-genders. To be feminist is to reject not only the
hierarchy of genders but of race-genders. To truly be antiracist
is to be feminist. To truly be feminist is to be antiracist.*

—Ibram X. Kendi, *How to Be an Antiracist* [30]

While the capture of many workplaces and corporations is a problem for adults and a general detriment to the meritocratic nature of America, the true aim is to impress these ideals upon young children. One reason for this, as stated by The Conscious Kid, is to make children aware of racial identities to promote a culture of "equity." However, it does not end there, as oppression "intersects" with other aspects of one's identity, such as gender, sex, sexual orientation, and all of the other "target identities" as we learned in the first course.

My course with Ulysses Smith had concluded, with many questions left unanswered. Exactly how does racism intersect with other forms of oppression? Is there a distinction between gender, sex, and sexuality? What is "Whiteness," and why does a good ally need to be "anti-racist"? After my beginner course, it was time to research deeper.

While these questions might seem mundane or downright trivial to some, billions of dollars of private and federal funds are invested into finding the answers, to little avail. In March 2022 during the Supreme Court confirmation hearings for Judge Ketanji Brown Jackson, she was asked a question by Senator Marsha Blackburn that billions of humans of all races, colors, and creeds have had no trouble answering as they sought to create families and ensure the survival of the human species. (Even drunk guys at a bar have a reported 98 percent success rates at distinguishing women from men. Or so I'm told.) As recounted in *USA Today*:

> In the 13th hour of Judge Ketanji Brown Jackson's confirmation hearing Tuesday, Sen. Marsha Blackburn, R-Tenn., asked the Supreme Court nominee: "Can you provide a definition for the word 'woman?'"
>
> Jackson, appearing confused, responded, "I'm not a biologist."
>
> Blackburn chided Jackson, claiming that "the fact that you can't give me a straight answer about something as fundamental as what a woman is underscores the dangers of the kind of progressive education that we are hearing about."[31]

Despite not being able to provide a definition of a woman, on April 7, 2022, Judge Jackson was confirmed by a vote of 53 to 47 to the Supreme Court.[32]

If a Supreme Court justice can't figure out what a woman or man is, what chance does a guy like me have? My degree isn't in gender studies, but I didn't let that stop me.

In late July 2022, I decided to enroll in "Gender and Sexuality: Diversity and Inclusion in the Workplace," taught by Dr. Susan Marine and Dr. Julie Beaulieu.[33]

Armed with a pencil and the remaining amounts of my fleeting sanity, I was immediately faced with an onslaught of vocabulary before I had even seen my professor's face. With the backdrop of a rainbow flag, we were presented with *ally, gay, intersex, rights, human, lesbian, cisgender, stereotype, asexual, free, homosexual, bisexual, transgender, equal, queer, sexism, identity,* and *LGBT.*

Some of these terms were fairly standard to me, as someone who's spent no small amount of time on the Internet and social media. Some were arguably the exact same—or so I had thought—like "gay" and the more clinically sounding "homosexual," while some seemed vague and contextual, like "equal." And "queer" was just as much an identity to some as it is a slur to others.

To break the confusion, Dr. Susan Marine—a middle-aged, stocky, blonde woman entered (I assume she was a woman, but I cannot be sure as no pronouns were given). She began outlining the scope of the course, and the knowledge we should have by the end of the month: gender, sex, sexuality, and the identities that compose the LGBTQIA+ community. Before I could question the utility of any of this information, we were informed that "Because we all live with gender expectations, this course is crucial for any profession and for understanding the world around us."[34] Very similar to my previous class, diversity was sold as universally applicable and as useful as a bottle of snake oil.

To assist her in the presentation, Dr. Julie Beaulieu, a very androgynous—woman?—with a baby face and neatly kept hair and glasses, wearing dingy and neutral gray attire joined in. Beaulieu detailed their shared academic history in the field of gender and sexuality studies, and went on to state something with which I agree—partially:

> As we hope to show, there is a direct relationship between theory and practice. How we think about gender and sexual difference shapes how we engage with ourselves and others. Thinking critically about gender and sexuality and being attuned to the social forces that shape different experiences is central to building inclusive workplaces and communities.[35]

There is indeed a relationship between theory and practice: praxis. As discussed in the previous chapter, praxis is the act of putting theory into practice, regardless of the validity of the theory itself. On its own, praxis is neither positive nor negative; it is dependent on the theory underpinning it. If the theory is: "People should not judge others based on intrinsic characteristics over which they have no control," then the implementation will likely yield non-discriminatory results. If, instead, the theory is: "Society is structured to support one group at the expense of the other, based on those intrinsic characteristics," one might expect increased tensions between these groups.

In the first week, we had to learn all our key terms because if you don't know the meaning of a word, how can you expect to understand someone else, or be understood yourself? In alphabetical order, we had to learn the meaning of *agender, androgynous, anti-miscegenation laws, asexual, benign variation, cisgender, gay, gender binary, hermaphrodite, heterosexual, homosexual, intersex, lesbian, queer, Romeo and Juliet exception, sex category, sex-positive movement, sexual orientation, trans,* and *transgender.*[36]

We were told that this was a comprehensive, but not exhaustive, list of terms. It begs the question then of how many genders there are, and where the line into absurdity lies. Are all these identities equally target or agent identities? Which omnipotent force is responsible for creating and maintaining so many different kinds of oppression?

I felt fairly comfortable with the definitions of most of the words, but there were a few that were new to me. For example, "agender" means that a person does not identity as either a man or woman. Okay, I get it: kind of like asexual.

Next up was "benign variation." I think I get the idea—a variation that doesn't matter much, either positive or negative—but I wanted to be sure that I understood, so I listened carefully. This definition came from the work of Gayle Rubin, who argued that sexuality might exist independently from racism and oppression. This idea has been viciously attacked by modern feminists and was presented to us as a form of wrong think, even though most feminists of the 1970s and 1980s would have agreed with it.

The only other term that confused me was the so-called "Romeo and Juliet exception." This exception refers to a series of laws in many states that specify that an individual over the age fourteen can consent to sex with another person, as long as that person is within three years of the first person's age. Boys being boys, and girls being girls, or maybe I should say non-binaries being non-binaries, that's probably a reasonable law.

It was not immediately apparent to me why a law on the age of consent was included in a course like this.

With all of our terms defined, we then moved to something a little less bitter sounding but perhaps more insidious, the "Genderbread person."

>»«

The class was presented with the graphic of a smiling gingerbread man cookie, and although the picture provided still looks exactly like a gingerbread man, there have been some modifications to his recipe.

The Genderbread Person v3.3

Gender is one of those things everyone thinks they understand, but most people don't. Like *Inception*. Gender isn't binary. It's not either/or. In many cases it's both/and. A bit of this, a dash of that. This tasty little guide is meant to be an appetizer for gender understanding. It's okay if you're hungry for more. In fact, that's the idea.

Identity

Attraction

Expression

Sex

For a bigger bite, read more at http://bit.ly/genderbread

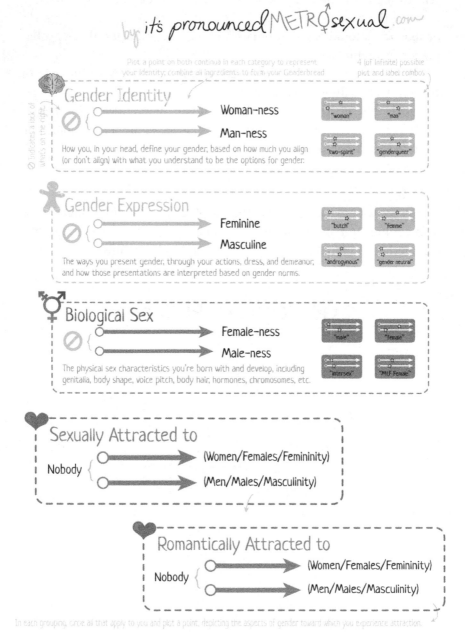

it's pronounced METROsexual.com

At the head we now have a brain, which was labeled "Identity."

In the chest we have a heart, which was labeled "Attraction."

The outline of the figure was titled "Expression."

The crotch area of the gingerbread man is now labeled "Sex" with a curious symbol which seems to be a combination of the traditional male, female, and a blend of the two symbols.

To help with understanding "gender identity" there are also arrows, which go from zero woman-ness to hyper-woman-ness, and from zero maleness to hyper-maleness.

To help with understanding "gender expression," these same arrows point to ultimate femininity and masculinity on the right.

To help with understanding "Anatomical Sex," there are arrows that show femaleness and maleness at the far right of the spectrum. Under these helpful arrows we are told:

Identity ≠ Expression ≠ Sex[37]

The core of the lesson is that gender identity resides in one's mind, sexuality and sexual attraction are a result of whom we love in our "heart," and our biological sex manifests as our sexual reproductive organs. Our outward appearance is how we express this identity.

Let's interpret *identity* as "how you wish to see yourself ideally," *expression* as "how you represent your inner identity to the world," and *sex* as "your primary sexual characteristics." Aside from the incredibly narcissistic or highly self-satisfied, most people have a disconnection between how they wish they were and how they are. Anyone maintaining a weight loss diet or exercise routine could tell you that. And for most of the population, their identity is linked to their physical sex. Most women do not want to have masculine appeal, and vice versa.

Gender ≠ Sexual Orientation[38]

Well, damn. I'm not certain if the organizers realize the weight of this statement on their ideology. Why is the "t" of "transgender" inextricably tied to the "lesbian, gay, and bisexual" demographics, if gender and sexual attraction are unrelated concepts? Do they mean to suggest that some women are more feminine than others without being lesbian, and the same is true of men with regard to masculinity and being gay? I would agree with that; I've met crossdressing men who would be confused if you called them women, and tomboys who would be insulted if you called them men.

But then it begs the question: why are surgery and drugs used to affirm an identity in one's own head?

I am also a little confused about the spectrum of "anatomical sex."

Humans generally come in one of two standard configurations, with a wide breadth of countries of origin, language, and color options.

In reality, the binary of sex exists down to every cell in the human body. Just because you don't look like or aspire to be the stereotype of a man or woman does not mean that biology is negated.

The presentation then divided sexual and romantic attraction into separate categories between "feminine or female people" or "masculine or male people", meaning that sometimes the two might not match.

Does that mean I could go to dinner with a woman for the romantic attraction, then leave her and have sex with some guy, or vice versa? How do these relationships function?

Dating is already difficult enough without considering that someone may be romantically interested in you yet hold no sexual feelings for you, while said person identifies as a "genderless masculine person with some female-ness." Again, I value mutual understanding, but words have to have solid meaning to achieve that. If any person can identify as a term, then the term has no boundary and is rendered meaningless. For example, no usable information is obtained from the description: a gay man who has a female anatomy and only sleeps with women, because "gay" means males attracted to men.

The final lesson of the week broke down the distinction between "sex" and "sex category," the latter being a term with which I was wholly unfamiliar. Beaulieu described "sex category" as "the biological facts and details that are used to classify individuals as male or female: reproductive organs, sexual organs, chromosomes, gonads, and hormones." Meaning, the physical manifestations of one's sexual characteristics.

"Sex" in this context is used as a purely legal term, used by governing bodies to track disparities across "legal males" and "legal females," the definition of which was subject to cultural norms, as was the age of consent.

> Today most US states have laws that require sexual actors to be between the ages of 16 to 18 to consent to sexual activity. But only a little less than 150 years ago the age of consent was between ten and 12 in most US states.
>
> I think we can all agree that age of consent laws are beneficial. What I am trying to highlight here is how they have changed over time and how they vary by cultural location.
>
> Societal norms define the legal age of consent.[39]

I wasn't quite sure what to make of the information I had just received. I had always understood that sex was the physical sexual traits of one's chromosomes, a view even shared by gender-critical activists a few years prior. But now it was relegated to a mere legal term with no definable connection to the people being labeled under it. And the aim of the course was to learn how to progress societal norms and become a progressive ally of the LGBTQIA+ community, was it not?

In that confusion, the first week ended.

I was no longer an intact individual—but like the genderbread person, I'd been broken into a bunch of cookie pieces, which couldn't be put back together.

»«

With the sweet interlude of our genderbread person over, we were to confront the horror of all horrors in next week's lesson: toxic masculinity and sex discrimination.

It began with Paul Carvel's Man Box theory.

We were told in tones of disapproval of the societal requirements to fit inside the Man Box: being tough, strong, non-emotional, decisive, physically imposing, verbally forceful, and having the ability to handle weaker or lesser others.[40]

The "outside the box" traits are sensitivity, kindness, vulnerability, openness, warmth, gentleness, fear, sadness, small physical stature, and quietness. According to Carvel, men are "expected to stay inside the box at all times" and "boys and men who do not conform may find themselves judged by peers, especially other boys and men, and may not be given access to certain kinds of power and privilege afforded to other men in society."[41]

This portrayal might be suitable for a child's stereotype of masculinity, but let's apply a bit more scrutiny. The traits considered within the Man Box are traits generally required to solve problems. Toughness and strength can be vital traits when engaged in a challenging or potentially dangerous task. The ability to set one's emotions aside and make rational, quick decisions is typically a defining trait of a good leader. If firemen arrived on the scene of a raging inferno and were overcome with emotion and unable to act, every lost second could be a life lost. Security guards who aren't able to deal with physical altercations will not be able to carry out their job duties.

On the other hand, Carvel's characterization of kindness, sadness, and sensitivity outside of the definition of masculinity is simply incorrect. Just as there are times to be strong and stoic, there are appropriate times to be vulnerable. Fathers who break down in tears because they are unable to see their children often receive extraordinary sympathy from other men, showing many traits outside the Man Box without condemnation.

Dr. Marine goes on to expand on this phenomenon, stating that this kind of man-on-man discrimination is "especially true for men who identify as gay because 'real men are supposed to be heterosexual', and even more so for those who transgress gender."[42]

I can't speak personally to the trans issue, but as a gay man who has always valued competence, it is a rare event to feel excluded because of my sexual orientation. However, this may be because I do not make my sexuality the most prominent part of my personality or identity. I have worked blue collar jobs in some of the most stereotypically masculine environments, where I don't have much input to add when the conversation consists of "butt vs. breasts" or "what's your type of woman?" Nevertheless, I have also been excluded from conversations about musical tastes or a local sports team's victory, which is due to my lack of knowledge not my sexuality.

None of this is discrimination; not everyone can be included in every conversation. It seemed to me that the model of masculinity presented by the Man Box theory is grounded in a very negative, archaic, and stereotyped view of masculinity, without contextualization of why some of these traits can be good or bad, depending on the situation. It also has the implication that men should not desire to be pillars of stability and strength for their loved ones as they have been for millennia across the entire world.

Moving on, Dr. Marine states that there is a similar cultural restriction on women, who are expected to be "focused on attractiveness, a slim figure, friendly, deferential to men without being too assertive or loud. Expected to be kind, warm and often smiling, traits associated with white women in particular."

These claims aren't true of Dr. Marine, sitting before us unsmiling and of stout proportions, boldly asserting and informing us of the ills of gendered expectations in society—yet why should she be less of a woman for it?

She explains that similar to the Man Box theory, women who fall outside these boundaries are similarly subjected to discrimination, especially in the case of "trans women" (biological men who live as women, often through surgery and drugs) who attempt to use a facility or join a space historically separated by biological sex. This discrimination can manifest itself in many forms, she says, from using the incorrect pronouns to legal exclusion from sex-segregated spaces. Once more, a bit of scrutiny calls the validity of these claims into dispute. As we learned earlier, *gender ≠ sex ≠ sex category*, so what is the rationale behind including men in female spaces, even if those men "identify" as women?

As the lesson neared its conclusion, my takeaway was that Western society has created rigid stereotyped categories for men and women, and being outside these stereotypes will incur societal judgment and discrimination. Therefore, these stereotypes should be not only rejected, but replaced with their opposite qualities.

However, without understanding why these stereotypes exist to begin with, or when these qualities might be beneficial, I was getting the message that there was a desired list of traits for men, and an undesired list.

The problem is that the unapproved list takes away the most useful traits of a man, turning him into the worst kind of woman, if that term still has a definition. Furthermore, women are to adopt the traits considered toxic in men.

»«

The next lesson covered lesbian, gay, and transgender issues in the workplace.

Dr. Marine explained that an understanding of gender and identity creates an enriched community aspect to any workplace setting, even though workplaces are typically places where such topics are irrelevant to the completion of the work tasks:

> Most of us rarely, if ever, discuss these important aspects of our identities with our co-workers. We may want to, but have been told they are irrelevant to the work we do, or even that talking about them is unprofessional. However, history has shown that people of different genders, sexes, and sexual orientations, who decide to be open about who they are, or who are labeled by co-workers as being different in some way, in the workplace, are sometimes treated differently in fact, discriminated against for doing so. This can be true just for showing up to work as who you are.[43]

Unless you were to show up to work dressed in rainbow clothing, with earrings or armbands displaying your pronouns and sexual orientation, I am not sure how others would be able to infer your new, chosen gender or sexuality. While there's nothing wrong with being different, it might very well be inappropriate in a variety of workplaces. A kindergarten teacher, for example, who insists on informing everyone around her of her sexual interests may raise some red flags, and rightfully so.

Dr. Marine expands on this concept, stating that the origin of such workplace practices has roots in the American slave trade, as racism, homophobia, and sexism are intrinsically linked to each other:

> Until the mid-1800s, virtually the only people who did paid work in the United States were white men. Women rarely held paid jobs unless they were domestic laborers, teachers, or nurses, and their wages were a paltry representation of what we might consider to be fair pay today. Black people living in the United States were held in slavery from the 1600s until they were symbolically freed by the emancipation proclamation. Decreed by President Abraham Lincoln in 1863. For many years afterward most lived in some form of indentured servitude, hard labor with very low pay, often designed to require them to buy their freedom. White men thus held most of the paid jobs and virtually all professional jobs in business, medicine, journalism, Government and other well paying fields.[44]

There's no doubt of injustice in the past, and a minority of people in the present surely hold biased views.

It is undeniable that in early American history most Blacks were kept out of the workforce until their emancipation, that segregation continued for many decades after that, and that White men had a virtual lock on well-paid positions. It is also true that for centuries women rarely held jobs outside of domestic laborers, teachers, or nurses and they received wages which were abysmally low.

However, what was not said was that as our freedom expanded and the discrimination of the past was outlawed and became culturally stigmatized, men and women of all ethnicities still often engage in traditional pursuits. In other words, men and women might be different on a fundamental level beyond socialization.

Men and women might value certain aspects of their lives differently, such as success in a career or the strength of their social relationships. Men may find themselves attracted more to careers that involve a specific intellectual or physical challenge, while women may find themselves attracted more to work that creates a social community. Women might also be less interested in jobs where the labor is strenuous or a danger to their long-term health if they want to be mothers in the future.

Let there be no mistake about what I'm saying: there must be complete freedom in the choices available to men and women.

But once the freedom is given, and the choices made, we must not criticize the outcomes of those choices if they do not result in a fifty-fifty split between men and women. Not all disparity is the result of discrimination.

»«

The question of the essential nature of men and women is a fascinating one which has occupied thinkers throughout the centuries.

And we may be getting an answer. Here is clinical psychologist, university professor, and bestselling author, Dr. Jordan Peterson, discussing the latest research in this area:

> In the last lecture, in Helsinki, it was Finland's Father's Day, I talked about masculine virtue. In Stockholm, I concentrated more on what has become known as the "gender paradox." Here is the paradox in a nutshell: as societies become more gender-equal in their social

and political policies, men and women become more different in certain aspects, rather than more similar...

Had you asked any group of social scientists, left-wing, centrist, conservative (if you could find them) ~30 years ago, "Will egalitarian social policies in wealthy countries produce men and women who are more similar or more different?" it is a certain bet that the majority would have said "more similar."[45]

This seems to be a commonly held belief, that generally men and women have the same set of values and goals. In many ways it's true, especially when one considers the average man and the average woman, but it's at the extremes where we start to differ, says Peterson:

First, men and women are more similar than they are different. This is true, cross-culturally. Even when men and women are most different—in those cultures where they differ most, and along those trait dimensions where they differ most—they are more similar than different. However, the differences that do exist are large enough that they play an important role in determining or at least affecting important life outcomes, such as occupational choice...

Where are the largest differences? Men are less agreeable (more competitive, harsher, tough-minded, skeptical, unsympathetic, critically minded, independent, stubborn). This is in keeping with their proclivity, also documented cross-culturally, to manifest higher rates of violence and antisocial or criminal behavior, such that incarceration rates for men vs. women is approximately fifteen to one.

Women are higher in negative emotion, or neuroticism. They experience more anxiety, emotional pain, frustration, grief, self-conscious doubt, and disappointment (something in keeping with their proclivity to experience depression at twice the rate of men). These differences appear to emerge at puberty. Perhaps it's a consequence of women's smaller size, and the danger that poses in conflict. Perhaps it's a consequence of their sexual vulnerability. Perhaps (and this is the explanation I favor) it's because women have always taken primary care of infants, who are exceptionally vulnerable, and must therefore suffer from hyper-vigilance to threat.[46]

As a man, I do not feel offended that Peterson correctly points out that the incarceration rate for men is fifteen times that of women. It's a simple, verifiable fact. A fact that results in inequity.

Does that mean we should have affirmative action to increase the proportion of women in prison? Of course not. But the average differences do not end there, as Peterson explains:

There are other sex differences, as well, but they aren't as large, excepting that of the aforementioned interest: men are comparatively more interested in things and women in people. This is the largest psychological difference between men and women yet identified. And these differences drive occupational choice, particularly at the extremes. Engineers, for example, tend to be those who are not only interested in things, but who are more interested in things than most people, *men or women.*

It's very important to remember that many choices are made at the extreme, and not the average. It's not the average more aggressive/less agreeable male that's in prison. In fact, if you draw a random man and a random woman from the population, and you bet that the woman is more aggressive/less agreeable, you'd be correct about 40% of the time. But if you walked into a roomful of people, everyone of whom had been selected to be the most aggressive person out of a 100, almost everyone of them would be male.[47]

This understanding of the agency of the individual versus the average trend of a demographic is crucial to understanding the concept of sexual dimorphism and the sexes' distribution in society. We no longer live in the era of the slave trade, nor in an age of the traditional domestic housewife. Much of the disparity in modern Western society is not a result of limited choices, it is a result of near unlimited choice.

Unfortunately, none of this nuance was brought up or even slightly addressed in our class. We were taught that it is only due to the advocacy of the women's rights movement in the 1960s and, by extension, LGBTQIA+ activists in the 1980s, that these groups were allowed to enter the workforce at all, and it is their continued activism that pushes women, as well as other historically marginalized groups toward equitable representation in the workforce against discrimination.

Americans need to speak honestly about the genuine problems in our society so that we can fix them. We also need to speak honestly about the tradeoffs between men and women.

If you group all men and women together, you will find that, as a group, men earn more money. However, men also work more hours than women,[48] often in physically demanding or dangerous roles. This accounts for most, if not all, the observed pay difference.

If you group all men and women together, you will find women live an average of four to seven years longer than men.

If you group all men and women together, you will find on average that women have more friends than men and stronger social connections.

What do you value more:

> Money?
> Years of life?
> Family?

Depending on your answer and temperament, you will most likely orient your life toward one of these goals at the expense of the others, because nobody can have it all. And to attempt to equalize all these results across sex, gender, and countless other identity labels would require restricting the accessible paths for individuals of any background.

In other words, to equalize outcome, some demographics will have to be promoted over others, and some will need to be restricted more than others. You can have equity, or you can have freedom of choice—not both.

Unfortunately, this entire side of the conversation is left out of the cultural discussion both in this lesson and wider society, as law and corporate structures are altered to facilitate equity. To bring our second week lesson to a close, Dr. Marine leaves us with this:

> ENDA [Employment Non-Discrimination Act] should be passed into law to ensure federal protection for all workers. And individual workplaces must commit to becoming LGBTQ friendly by sponsoring training and education for employees and having policies which protect workers internally from harassment and other forms of disadvantage.
>
> Johnson and Johnson, Macy's and Pfizer all feature strong commitments to transgender inclusion in the workplace. According to the HRC Corporate Equality Index. Positive change is happening, but much more work needs to be done. We'll continue to talk more in-depth about the ways that gender, sex, and sexual orientation discrimination play out in the workplace. And what we can do as individuals and communities to prevent and address it.[49]

>«

In the third week, I began to fully grasp the true purpose and meaning of what it meant to be a "good ally" to the LGBTQIA+ community.

This week, Dr. Beaulieu began with the concept of sexuality as a theory. She began with the declaration that most of the world is highly invested in sex, and the large volume of work dedicated to sexuality across the world proves this to be true. Thus, we were going to be examining sexuality with reference to religious discourse, medicinal discourse, and popular discourse. According to her, sexuality is often framed with religious perspectives even when presented in a medical context, meaning that the entire concept needs to be reframed to address the subject accurately.

While I can appreciate the desire to address a subject in isolation of other influences, what she said next made me question everything I had learned, not only in this course, but about the entire history and goal of LGBTQIA+ activism:

> Collectively, this discourse establishes the meaning and function of sexuality in our lives. Much like theories of gender and theories of other social categories like race and ethnicity, *theories of sexuality have abandoned simplistic, essentialist theories of sexuality, theories that root difference in the body or nature. This is what we might call a "born this way" theory of sexuality. Biological essentialism assumes that people are born gay or straight.* Typically, essentialism leaves very little variation outside of the binary. It also assumes that our sexuality will stay the same throughout our lives because of an innate biological fixed nature.[50] (Emphasis added.)

It was as if I could hear the scratch of a record, or the shattering of glass as a speeding car collided with a flaming dumpster.

I'm a gay Black man. I'm not gay because I was convinced to be this way; I can look to my past, which suggests that there is an aspect of nature to what determined my sexuality. The basis of the movement for gay acceptance is that homosexual people, much like heterosexuals, did not choose their sexuality, and thus it is wrong to discriminate against an inherent characteristic. The same philosophy echoed from the civil rights movement: Judging people on inherent characteristics is wrong and intolerable.

What does it mean that gender and sexuality theorists want to abandon any notion of a biological essentialist view? Are they proposing to deny my own lived experience, as well as the lives of other gays and lesbians who are adamant that they are naturally attracted to the same sex? Before I could fully comprehend, Dr. Beaulieu continued:

> In the late 20th century, sociologists and anthropologists introduced the idea that sexuality is a learned behavior. Cross-cultural and subcultural sexual practices showcase a wide range of different sexual patterns, interests, and ideas. *These theories are called social constructionist theories, and they primarily focus on the social forces that produce our sexual tastes and interests. Other social theories, like Marxism and feminism, introduce the relationship between sexuality and society.* Marxists look at the relationship between economic structures and patterns, arguing that the economy is a key factor in the development of sexual norms.[51] (Emphasis added.)

Because, of course, what fun could sex possibly be without a dash of Marxism? I suppose it could suit a sadist who enjoys watching the suffering of others at his own hand. And that hand was showing from inside the Trojan horse of gender and sexuality studies.

Marxism is a broadly used term that encompasses a range of political, social, and economic theories that originate with nineteenth-century radical German philosophers Karl Marx and Friedrich Engels. From Maoism in China to Marxism-Leninism and Trotskyism in Russia to the Khmer Rouge in Cambodia—each time these theories are adopted, tens of millions of bodies are left in the wake of the countries they destroy.[52]

The running theme of a Marxist ideology is the ever-present class conflict, where a higher class keeps a lower class down to maintain its own power and privilege. In the exact same way that we were taught about "agent" identities and "target" identities in the previous course, we are now told to believe that some people, due to their race or, in this case, because of their sex, sexuality, and gender are more oppressed than others.

But that's not the only objective. The lunacy continued:

> Like other identity-based social movements, including the feminist movement and the civil rights movement, the gay liberation movement has frequently relied on the idea of a natural homosexual, someone who is born different and someone who deserves rights based on this natural and thus, unavoidable difference. Gay historians have challenged this belief, arguing that the very idea of homosexuality is a relatively recent invention. We will explore this idea further in the lecture on the history of sexual identity. Queer theorists take a radical social constructionist approach to sexuality...
>
> One of the largest claims about sexuality by queer theorists is about the stability of identity itself. What does it mean to be gay, or to have a sexuality? *By destabilizing categories and identities, queer theorists challenge the idea of a natural or normal order of things.*[53] (Emphasis added.)

And there was the final piece of this rainbow puzzle: by rejecting the idea that sexuality is inherent, one opens the door to socially engineering the sexuality of others. If society at large adopts the custom of rejecting traditional views on sex and sex practices, it sees the normalization of non-traditional families, or the destruction of the family unit altogether. If sexuality can be "learned," a practice once called conversion therapy, then it might be possible to convince straight or gay people into sexual acts with trans-identifying people of the sex they're not originally attracted to.

Radical queer theorists reject the "born this way" argument for sexuality (Lady Gaga must be so disappointed that her 2011 song of that name has now become just another example of right-wing hate). This is crazy when one considers what gay rights activists endured in the 1950s and 1960s when police would regularly raid their bars, or someone could be arrested for having gay sex. I'd like to have it explained to me how somebody in those times "learned" this sexual way of being, which involved a life of secrecy, shame, and the ever-present fear of discovery and social shunning. I'm sure that many of my readers of a certain age will recall a gay friend, when he or she came out, saying if there was any way they could have been straight, they would have chosen it because it would have been so much easier for their lives.

But they could not deny who they were.

The "born this way" argument for sexuality was the initial argument in pursuit of gay acceptance, built on the successful civil rights campaign of Martin Luther King, Jr., declaring that Blacks did not choose their race, and that everybody was entitled to his or her God-given freedom. In this formulation, gay men and lesbians, did not choose their sexuality any more than Black people chose their race. As consenting adults, gay men and lesbians should have the same right as everybody in the straight world to live, cohabitate, and marry the person of their choice.

In conversation with my straight friends on issues of sexuality, they express the same feeling I have, namely that before anybody told me what my orientation should be, I knew.

The question that needs to be asked of the LGBTQIA+ activists is: if you believe that sexuality is a social construct, what purpose do these Drag Queen Story Hours for children have, other than to influence their sexual conditioning? It is difficult to see these "story hours" as anything other than an attempt to groom children into certain sexual lifestyles. And these are not isolated incidents restricted to progressive cities, schools from Missouri to NYC are subjecting children to sexually explicit performances, often without parental consent.[54], [55]

> New York City Mayor Eric Adams defended Thursday sending drag queens to public schools and libraries, saying that inviting flamboyant female impersonators to read to young children promotes "a love of diversity."
>
> The mayor's statement came a few days after the New York Post reported that the city had paid $207,000 to Drag Story Hour NYC to read books to students at dozens of elementary schools, middle schools and high schools since 2018.
>
> "At a time when our LGBTQ+ communities are under increased attack across this country, we must use our education system to educate," Mr. Adams said.
>
> The goal is not only for our children to be academically smart, but also emotionally intelligent. Drag storytellers, and the libraries and schools that support them, are advancing a love of diversity, personal expression, and literacy that is core to what our city embraces," he explained.[56]

Do you think I'm making too strong of a claim? That I'm perhaps a bit alarmist? This was part of my reading homework in the final week of that course—in "Thinking Sex: Notes for a Radical Theory of the Politics of Sexuality," Gayle Rubin wrote in 1984:

> The laws produced by the child porn panic are ill-conceived and misdirected. They represent the far-reaching alterations in the regulation of sexual behavior and abrogate important sexual civil liberties. But hardly anyone noticed as they swept through Congress and state legislatures. With the exception of

the North American Man/Boy Love Association and American Civil Liberties Union, no one raised a peep of protest.

The experience of art photographer Jacqueline Livingston exemplifies the climate created by the child porn panic. An assistant professor of photography at Cornell University, Livingston was fired in 1978 after exhibiting pictures of male nudes which included photographs of her seven-year-old son masturbating... It is easy to see someone like Livingston as a victim of the child porn wars. It is harder for most people to sympathize with actual boy-lovers. Like communists and homosexuals in the 1950s, boy-lovers are so stigmatized that it is difficult to find defenders for their civil liberties, let alone their erotic orientation.[57]

It was genuinely stomach-churning to read this. We're supposed to feel sorry for this sick woman who took pictures of her seven-year-old son masturbating and made them public?

In today's modern world one can be criminally prosecuted for the act of revenge porn (publicly distributing erotic pictures of a former partner), as this is universally acknowledged to be a violation of trust in the most intimate relationships. However, in revenge porn images, adults at least consented to the making of these erotic images.

In the case of a seven-year-old boy, there is no legal possibility of consent. And how were these images obtained? It seems doubtful that these images were taken in secrecy, which can only leave the likelihood that the boy's mother directed him in these acts. Under current laws, this woman should not have only lost her job, but should have been prosecuted for child abuse, and hopefully spent many years in prison, as well as forever be prevented from being around children.

Yet, we are supposed to feel sorry for the masturbation-procuring mother as a springboard for considering the plight of "boy-lovers."

This entirely distorted form of diversity and inclusion is being used as a cover for depravity and child abuse.

How can any person with the slightest of concern for children be comfortable with the idea of "boy-lovers?" It's akin to saying, "Well, cannibalism is a gastronomic orientation, and if you cross the line like serial killer, Jeffrey Dahmer, maybe we should punish you. But otherwise, we think people should feel free to express their cannibalistic orientation, free of social shaming."

A civilization needs to have lines that should not be crossed; without such lines it ceases to be a cohesive civilization with law and order.

The sexual abuse, grooming, and medical sterilization (which we will go into later) of children should be one of those lines. That should not be a left vs. right, or progressive vs. conservative issue. It is a question of pure right and wrong.

3

WON'T YOU PLEASE *STOP* THINKING OF THE CHILDREN?

We're raising a whole generation who regard facts as more or less, optional. We have kids in elementary schools who are being urged to take stands on political issues, to write letters to congressmen and presidents about nuclear energy. Not a decade old, and they're being thrown these kind of questions that can absorb the lifetime of a very brilliant and learned man.

They're being taught that it's important to have views, and they're not being taught it's important to know what you're talking about. It's important to hear the opposite viewpoint, and more important, learn to distinguish why viewpoint A and viewpoint B are different, and which has the most evidence and logic behind it.

—Thomas Sowell, *Economic Facts and Fallacies*[58]

The more I learned how to be an appropriate ally, the more I likened it to being an accomplice in a grand crime. Through my inclusive and diverse courses, I learned that the end goal of "queer theory" and LGBTQIA+ activism is to deconstruct and destabilize norms around sex, while also introducing children into this sexual revolution. In addition, the goal of creating "anti-racist" institutions and spaces is to generate race and gender equity activists from them.

What exactly is an anti-racist activist? And why is it important enough to warrant my employer to instruct its employees to develop product development guidelines around it? How does "anti-racism" compare to "racism"? To the average person, it sounds like the former would mean "to be against discrimination based on race or ethnicity," a concept supported by the average American. That, however, is not the woke or progressive definition of "anti-racism;" in fact it's the complete antithesis.

"Anti-racism" is a *very* ideologically loaded term that I can best define as: to support ideas, policies, and actions that support positive discrimination to encourage and uphold power equity across all marginalized identity groups. The term itself was created by Ibram X. Kendi, author of the book *How to Be an Antiracist*, in which he defines an antiracist as: "One who is expressing the idea that racial groups are equals and none needs developing, and is supporting policy that reduces racial inequity."[59] While we can agree that members of different races should be on equal standing in society and before the law, this will not result in an even distribution throughout society.

In practice, anti-racism is the use of positive or negative discrimination to achieve "equity" (meaning equal outcomes) among identity groups. This may take the form of awarding preferential treatment to marginalized or "target" identity groups, or creating spaces where perceived target identities have increased and exert disproportional influence over agent identities. These two definitions are so vastly different, it makes it difficult to facilitate conversations about the topic, and more important, difficult to criticize the ideology of anti-racism. Without understanding the progressive definition, it's very easy for someone accused of being racist to defend himself by proclaiming to be anti-racist, and that is the intent behind the term. After all, if you don't want to be called a racist, then you must be anti-racist, right? Kendi writes:

> We cannot be antiracist if we are homophobic or transphobic. We must continue to "affirm that all Black lives matter," as the co-founder of Black Lives Matter, Opal Tometi, once said.

> [...]

> To be queer antiracist is to serve as an ally to transgender people, to intersex people, to women, to the non-gender-conforming, to homosexuals, to their intersections, meaning listening, learning, and being led by their equalizing ideas, by their equalizing policy campaigns, by their power struggle for equal opportunity.[60]

The linguistic trap of progressive anti-racism is an attempt to manipulate those unaware of the ideology into being unwitting followers of its tenants, but also serves to subtly destroy the American ideal of colorblindness; not judging others based on their color or creed, but by their character.

Why? If individuals treat each other without regard to race or gender, then inequity between identity groups cannot be addressed as a problem. If inequity isn't a problem, then there is no justification to discriminate in order to create equity between identity groups. Colorblindness seeks to minimize the racial judgments between individuals to promote equality; anti-racism seeks to maximize the racial judgments between identity groups to promote equity. As Kendi says: "The most threatening racist movement is not the alt right's unlikely drive for a White ethnostate but the regular American's drive for a 'race-neutral' one."[61]

Despite anti-racism being used to advocate and reintroduce discrimination in America and, by extension, much of the developed Western world, it has become a fixture (or tumor) in virtually all of our cultural institutions from the highest offices of government to the homework lessons of grade-school children.

In Cupertino, California, a whistleblower came forward to denounce and call attention to the material being presented to third-graders. During a supposed math class, students were tasked with creating an "identity map," listing out their different identity labels, such as race, class, gender, and religion. The teacher went on to explain that those who identified with "white, middle class, cisgender, Christian and English" (agent identities) belonged to the dominant culture in America, thus holding more power and privilege than others. The students were then instructed to read aloud from *This Book is Anti-Racist: 20 Lessons on How to Wake Up, Take Action, and Do the Work*, a *New York Times* bestseller for teaching children about "anti-racism."[62]

In June 2020, a school district in western Oregon made a public declaration in response to the death of George Floyd, stating the following:

> Now, therefore be it resolved on this 8th day of June 2020, by the Board of the Tigard-Tualatin School District, that, the district condemns racism, racial violence, white supremacy, hate speech, and bigotry in all forms inside and outside of our schools; and,
>
> The district will work to be actively anti-racist and dismantle systemic racism in our schools and empower people of color.[63]

This kind of indoctrinatory education is not restricted to blue states and progressive cities. In Springfield, Missouri, teachers at Cherokee Middle School have undergone training to properly understand "diversity." The teachers must watch a nine-minute silent film showing the death of George Floyd with editorial commentary overlaid onto it.[64] Race activists used George Floyd's death to emotionally manipulate and justify much of their activism, rioting and other violence, and cultural crusade. Once the emotional framing is set, the teachers are introduced to topics such as oppression, systemic racism, and white supremacy, and are tasked with locating themselves on an "oppression matrix."

During the training, white supremacy is broken down between overt, socially unacceptable expressions, and covert, socially accepted expressions. According to the chart provided, a few aspects of socially accepted, covert white supremacy include:

- Colorblindness
- White silence
- Claiming "reverse-racism"
- Prioritizing White voices as experts
- Not believing experiences of "Black, Indigenous, and people of color" (BIPOC)
- Calling the police on Black people
- "All Lives Matter"

Both training documents from Cherokee Middle School emphasize the oppressor vs. oppressed class dynamic, and how White people (and those perceived to be White) are the beneficiaries of privilege at the expense of all other racial and ethnic groups. This is the concept of "White privilege" in praxis. Claiming that "White silence" and "reverse racism" is also a facet of white supremacy is a method of silencing dissent, while ensuring that those who buy into the framework are constantly and actively supporting anti-racist causes as "allies."

Children are growing up in a society where they are being taught that *not* considering race in their daily interactions with other people is wrong. They are being groomed to support the causes and political positions of misleadingly named organizations such as Black Lives Matter, while being told that even criticizing the organization is a form of upholding and reinforcing white supremacy and "White culture."

And what exactly is White culture? According to the Smithsonian's National Museum of African American History and Culture (NMAAHC):

> Whiteness and white racialized identity refer to the way that white people, their customs, culture, and

beliefs operate as the standard by which all other groups are compared. Whiteness is also at the core of understanding race in America. Whiteness and the normalization of white racial identity throughout America's history have created a culture where non-white persons are seen as inferior or abnormal.[65]

The NMAACH explains the components of White culture in a graphic on its website titled "Aspects & Assumptions of Whiteness & White Culture in the United States."[66]

ASPECTS & ASSUMPTIONS OF WHITENESS & WHITE CULTURE IN THE UNITED STATES

White dominant culture, or **whiteness**, refers to the ways white people and their traditions, attitudes and ways of life have been normalized over time and are now considered standard practices in the United States. And since white people still hold most of the institutional power in America, we have all internalized some aspects of white culture — including people of color.

Rugged Individualism
- The individual is the primary unit • Self-reliance
- Independence & autonomy highly valued + rewarded
- Individuals assumed to be in control of their environment, *"You get what you deserve"*

Family Structure
- The nuclear family: father, mother, 2.3 children is the ideal social unit
- Husband is breadwinner and head of household
- Wife is homemaker and subordinate to the husband
- Children should have own rooms, be independent

Emphasis on Scientific Method
- Objective, rational linear thinking
- Cause and effect relationships
- Quantitative emphasis

History
- Based on Northern European immigrants' experience in the United States
- Heavy focus on the British Empire
- The primacy of Western (Greek, Roman) and Judeo-Christian tradition

Protestant Work Ethic
- Hard work is the key to success
- Work before play
- "If you didn't meet your goals, you didn't work hard enough"

Religion
- Christianity is the norm
- Anything other than Judeo – Christian tradition is foreign
- No tolerance for deviation from single god concept

THE DIVERSITY CON

Status, Power & Authority
- Wealth = worth
- Your job is who you are
- Respect authority
- Heavy value on ownership of goods, space, property

Future Orientation
- Plan for future
- Delayed gratification
- Progress is always best
- "Tomorrow will be better"

Time
- Follow rigid time schedules
- Time viewed as a commodity

Aesthetics
- Based on European culture • Steak and potatoes; "bland is best"
- Woman's beauty based on blonde, thin – "Barbie"
- Man's attractiveness based on economic status, power, intellect

Holidays
- Based on Christian religions
- Based on white history & male leaders

Justice
- Based on English common law
- Protect property & entitlements
- Intent counts

Competition
- Be #1
- Win at all costs
- Winner/loser dichotomy
- Action Orientation
- Master and control nature
- Must always "do something" about a situation
- Aggressiveness and Extroversion
- Decision-Making
- Majority rules (when Whites have power)

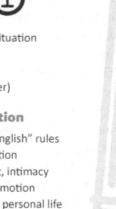

Communication
- "The King's English" rules
- Written tradition
- Avoid conflict, intimacy
- Don't show emotion
- Don't discuss personal life
- Be polite

"White culture" itself refers to attributes derived from the philosophy and ethos of the United States of America—individual liberty, meritocracy, and negative rights, as well as the Judeo-Christian values that are engraved into the history and culture of this country. Whether you are religious or not, the core of anti-racism—and by extension critical race theory (CRT)—is in direct opposition to the values of the United States of America.

Some of these attributes are ascribed to Whiteness because they are derived from core American philosophies (individualism and justice stem from the idea of liberty; competition and a strong work ethic relate to a focus on meritocracy; private property rights stem from the concept of negative rights). Other traits, however—punctuality, future-orientation, living in a nuclear family—are fundamental to maturity, success, and long-term happiness. Without managing one's time and planning for the future, the likelihood of achieving success becomes less and less realistic and more dependent purely on luck. Furthermore, if notions like "objective, rational thinking" and "understanding cause and effect" are traits of dominant White culture, are non-White cultures then to be associated with irrationality, short-sightedness and instant gratification? To segregate these qualities as "White" is to hold an exceptionally low view of non-White cultures and individuals. It ignores the achievements of many successful Black Americans, many of whom stand at the top of their respective industries, while setting up non-White children for failure—in school and in life.

The assumptions about the nuclear family being an aspect of Whiteness are particularly insidious. The stable family unit, with the biological parents raising their children, is the most ideal environment in which to raise a child. Not only in quality and financial stability of family life, but stable families serve the important function of cultivating the future prospects of their children. Academic achievement, mental stability, psychological maturation—all these factors that can help to achieve a better life are linked to strong family units during child development.

As if this was not bad enough, the propaganda with which children are being besieged is not limited to race.

»«

With the second course under my belt, I had learned much, but I still did not feel like an adequate ally of diversity and inclusion initiatives.

From *Diversity, Equity, and Inclusion: A Beginner's Guide*, we'd learned that the aim of DEI initiatives is to transform institutions into spaces where race, sex, gender, and alleged privilege are considered in hiring, promotion, and overall workplace and school culture. We understood that to an activist, "equity"—the equalizing of outcomes—was more important than a meritocratic system of "equality" because minorities supposedly can't be successful without the extra help. In a previous era, this same mindset was called "the White Man's Burden" owing to a poem by a British novelist in 1899, who expressed that it was the job of the White people to manage the other races, whom were thought inferior.[67] And the methods of creating such a culture involved converted HR trainings and volunteer employee groups that label all inequality as a result of discrimination.

After the "Gender and Sexuality: Diversity and Inclusion in the Workplace" course, we'd learned that sex and sexuality are entirely divorced from gender, which exists in the mind of the individual. And while most people regard sexuality as mostly inherent nature, the goal of the LGBTQIA+ movement is to redefine societal norms around sex and gender roles, and to destigmatize and normalize sexual behaviors and taboos. Much like DEI initiatives, this destabilization is often performed through HR training and redefinition of workplace guidelines to enforce respect and acceptance of alternative gender behavior.

This left one major institution in a bit of a blind spot: what about schools? For employers and employees, these strategies apply to transform their professional space into an inclusive and diverse zone. But what about classrooms? What does an inclusive classroom look like, and how is one created? Most importantly, what is the effect on the students?

For answers, I sought the instruction of another professional, and in September 2022, found myself enrolled in "Queering the Schoolhouse: LGBTQ+ Inclusion for Educators" offered by the University of Colorado.

Like any other class, it began with an introduction by each professor, whom we'd become acquainted with over the six-week length of the course. The first instructor was Dr. Jacob McWilliams, who boasted quite the resume as the director of the Gender and Sexuality Center and the director of the Women & Gender Center—both at the University of Colorado Anschutz Medical Campus in Denver—with a PhD in education and a concentration in gender, sexuality, and policy studies from Indiana University:

> I identify as a queer transgender man. I'm also white, non-disabled, formally educated and a U.S. citizen. All of these identities intersect in a wide variety of ways in my professional and personal life. I experience privilege because of some of these identities, and I have experienced oppression, harassment, discrimination, and marginalization because of other of these identities.[68]

I was undoubtedly in the right place, learning from someone with credentials like that.

The next instructor was Daryl Boyd, a middle-aged man with a shining bald head, graying beard with slightly effeminate mannerisms. Introducing himself with "he/him" pronouns, he announced himself as a masters student at the University of Colorado Denver in the Learning Design and Technology program, while also involved in the university's LGBTQIA+ inclusion program for educators, which I was enrolled in.[69]

The final instructor was Indiana University graduate Dr. Suraj Uttamchandani, pronounced Ut-um-che-nah-knee, which he made sure to articulate, stating that his name's proper pronunciation is very important to him as it reflects his heritage and culture—just like his "he/him" pronouns. In his working experience, Dr. Uttamchandani spent a lot of time working with LGBTQIA+ youth groups, and such groups were also the subject of his doctoral dissertation.[70]

With introductions, formalities, and pronouns out of the way, it was time to learn how to turn a schoolhouse "queer." Week one concluded with an explanation on terms, pronouns, and why they're important. Boyd explained that most people use pronouns in a manner that presumes the gender of the other person based on outward appearance. In doing so, it sends a potentially harmful message that individuals must look a certain way to identify with a certain gender.

Two problems with that. First, one's outward appearance is called "gender expression" as we'd learned from an earlier course on DEI. If you dress as a man (a masculine gender expression, in DEI terms), how the hell is anyone supposed to know what's really going on in your head? The ability to read minds would be helpful, but if I could do that, I'd have 1,000 more important uses for it than figuring out the title someone wants to go by.

Second problem: What harm is caused by being misgendered? Is it nebulously defined emotional harm, or a legal standard definition? If it's the latter, suggesting potential legal implications for not knowing every person's "x-e/x-em/x-ers" pronouns would leave the general public in a state of constant fear. Nobody can even quantify the number of genders that allegedly exist.

>«

Week two began with the answer to my long-held question on how to be a good ally, and apparently, being an ally wasn't even good enough. Boyd began his lecture with the following definitions:

> An *ally* is someone who acts and speaks on behalf of a marginalized, or disadvantaged person, or community, and is always accountable to that person or community. To hold this title, it is received when the person or community the individual is working for acknowledges their efforts.

> *Accomplices* however, are those who join in solidarity with marginalized people, actively working for their cause. Accomplices are those you find linked arm in arm with you in the streets, to bring attention to your cause. They fight against the systemic and systematic oppression, intentionally designed and implemented to keep the marginalized suppressed. "The difference between an ally and an accomplice, is the difference between standing for LGBTQ plus people, and standing with them."
>
> *Advocates*, on the other hand are those who support marginalized communities from privileged positions, working directly with those marginalized groups.[71]

When people seek allies, it's usually because they're engaging in a conflict of some kind. When they seek accomplices, it typically implies some kind of criminal or nefarious action. Maybe there is something inherently wrong with teaching children about sexuality after all, and the activists know it.

To reinforce my growing suspicion, the week's required reading was "LGBTQ+ Youth Expertise on Allyship and Advocacy for Educators," an article by Dr. Uttamchandani in June 2019. In the article, Uttamchandani recounts how he worked in a "progressive stronghold in the conservative Midwest" to establish a youth LGBTQIA+ group under the pseudonym "Chroma" in an unidentified town under the pseudonym "Bricksburg."

One would think if he was so proud of this work, the use of pseudonyms would not be necessary to "protect" this organization or its work. If it is not a matter of honest work but malicious subversion requiring the use of accomplices and allies, the need for secrecy makes more sense.

In Chroma, the aim was to create youth educators to teach about the topic of LGBTQIA+ cultural competence and equity. These youth educators, aged twelve to twenty, go on to advocate and "educate their fellow students" in their schools, advocating policy changes to create an inclusive environment for marginalized students. The focus of Chroma's educational work is on the intersections of "gender and sexual non-conformity" and the "adult/youth binary." According to Chroma, "heteronormativity" itself must be uprooted to create a space where LGBTQIA+ acceptance can be created:

> In our own work together as Chroma, we must dismantle heteronormativity and its related social constructs—patriarchy, homophobia, transphobia, heterosexism, genderism, and sexism. We work to uproot these from our own thinking and ways of interacting, while bringing them into the educational trainings as content.[72]

Anyone who's spent any time in a progressive political discussion has heard these words rattled off, often in the same copied-and-pasted order and diction. The focus of the group was not to help LGBTQIA+ youth to create more tolerant classrooms, but to turn them into child activists for a loose collection of Marxist identity-based political theory. Another Trojan horse to teach through praxis.

Week three of the training began with "Learning While Queer: A History of LGBTQ+ People in Schools" and opened with some claims about the history of gay education in America, using the Anoka-Hennepin school district in Minnesota as an example. Beginning with an AIDS curriculum in the mid-1980s through the hiring of a transgender music teacher in 1998, Uttamchandani concludes with the tragic suicide of seven bullied students, some of whom were gay. From this timeline, he said, we can make a few conclusions about LGBTQIA+ history. First: LGBTQIA+ students are not new; second, queer lives are mostly made visible through health crises and suicide; and third, schools have historically failed to support and protect LGBTQIA+ students.[73]

While any loss of life is a tragedy, particularly young lives who have not yet experienced the world, there's a major problem with this claim: not all of the seven bullied children who committed suicide were reportedly gay. Assuming that all these deaths were the result of bullying (a tall claim by itself), the bullying wasn't entirely based on sex or gender identity, if at all. Despite that, we're expected to take this specific case as the rule and lived experience for gay youth in all schools. It felt more like these deaths were being unjustly exploited for an agenda, because the correlation and conclusion were so terribly disjointed, and unfortunately it wouldn't be the last time hearing that unsubstantiated claim about LGBTQIA+ youths and suicide.

The class then switches to the next section, hopefully titled "It Gets Better? The Current Climate For LGBTQ+ Students," where we're told the following:

> So, let's return to the statistic: 34.8% of LGBTQ+ students missed at least one entire day of school in the past month because they felt unsafe or uncomfortable. A deficit approach would treat these students as broken and in need of repair. It would blame students for not coming to school, even though doing so would feel or be unsafe. A deficit approach would then solve this problem by asking students to try acting straight or to not come out in schools. Deficit approaches can feel reasonable to us, but they position students rather than schools as in need of change. By contrast, a resource approach would legitimize the student by hearing the student, affirming their [sic] feelings and recognizing that their [sic] LGBTQ+ identity is meaningful and valuable. Teachers taking a resource perspective would go on to ask, what factors make the school feel uncomfortable to students? Like bullying, harmful teacher behavior, and exclusionary policies. They would work collaboratively with students and administrators to solve these problems at the school-wide level.[74]

What exactly is a *deficit approach*? It's a teaching style where student backgrounds are seen as obstacles to be overcome and that asks children to minimize their cultural experience in order to succeed. The lesson claims this to be the view of traditional American schools. By contrast, a resource-based or asset-based approach understands that students come from various backgrounds, and that those backgrounds can support learning. Ironically, the example we were given made an excellent case for why not to use this new method. To demonstrate a deficit-learning approach, we're given the example of a child who speaks Mandarin Chinese at home, and thus experiences difficulty with English in class. The "deficit" comes from asking the child to suppress his or her heritage and cultural language while learning English. Instead, having the teacher note that "learning Mandarin can be useful" and playing to the child's strength is a more asset-based approach. The problem is that the latter method does not help the child to learn English any better, a skill that people need to function maximally in an English-speaking country. The approach pejoratively labeled as "deficit" is the only approach that identifies the problem and addresses it. The other is lazy compassion masked as empathy and understanding.

In an attempt to further ground these misleading statements, Uttamchandani presents the class with a self-reported online survey with a pool of 27,000 respondents, with stats such as:

- 1 in 10 respondents who were out about being transgender to their immediate family reported that a family member was violent to them because they were transgender. 8% reported they were kicked out for being transgender.
- 54% of respondents who were out, or perceived as transgender, reported experiencing harassment while in school (K–12). 13% reported experiencing sexual assault, 24% reported experiencing physical assault because they were transgender.[75]

A major problem with this survey is that it's based entirely on the *perceived* intent behind the various negative events a person might experience throughout his life. Perception, unlike what is taught by gender activists, does not equate to reality.

For a lot of people, for a lot of reasons, growing up is hard. I have known some straight, White men who were horribly bullied in school, some due to their actions, others through no fault of their own. I had not yet discovered my sexuality in middle school or high school, and was still bullied harshly for any number of other reasons.

Uttamchandani made no attempt to justify or verify these figures. It is entirely possible that some or many of these issues, such as being evicted, have to do with age, cleanliness, not paying rent, or mental health issues causing instability in the home, rather than with gender identity. The survey results presented to us about the physical and mental health of transgender youth continued:

- 39% of respondents reported experiencing serious psychological distress in the month prior to the survey, compared to only 5% of the wider US population.
- 40% of respondents reported having attempted suicide in their lifetime, almost 10x higher than the general US population. 7% attempted suicide in the past year, compared to 0.6% of the US population.
- 55% of respondents who sought coverage for transition-related surgery in the past year were denied, and 25% of those who sought coverage for hormones in the past year were denied.[76]

Leaving aside the question of whether this self-reported data is an accurate snapshot of the health of transgender people in society, let's make some comparisons for perspective. The reported suicide rate of transgender people in America appears to be higher than the suicide rates of American slaves before the Civil War, or Jews in Nazi concentration camps.[77] With that in mind, are we supposed to believe that society's non-acceptance of chosen gender identities of children in the 21st century, in the most prosperous country in human existence, means that these children have a worse quality of life than did slaves?

It's more plausible to believe that the transgender identity is often a manifestation of deeper mental problems, or a misguided escape from them.

To determine which is more likely to be true, we could look at a relatively recent population of individuals who had undergone gender-reassignment surgery to see if it resulted in a decrease in their use of mental health services.

A 2020 article in the *American Journal of Psychiatry*, however, found that gender-reassignment surgery *did not* result in the patients receiving fewer mental health services.[78]

Meaning: surgery and hormones did not seem to improve their mental issues.

It seems that the failure of gender-reassignment surgery to fix the perception of being in the wrong body, and the accompanying mental health issues, is something that should be a vital part of the conversation, and not regarded as a bigoted attack rooted in hatred. Perhaps it is mentally damaging to raise children as the opposite sex, and if the goal is to prevent suicides, we must work with all the data and speak honestly.

»«

By the start of week four of the training, the instructors must have believed that we were mentally broken down, so it was time to rebuild us as freshly minted social justice warriors with the presentation titled "Contemporary Practices in LGBTQ+ Inclusion." Uttamchandani began with a discussion of "safe spaces":

> **Safe space:** A supportive and intentionally affirming environment for LGBTQ+ students. In a safe space, educators hold the dual task of controlling classroom environments and being an advocate on behalf of LGBTQ+ students. Educators are also direct actors

responsible for implementing LGBTQ+ content in class curricula.

You might recognize some of the components of the Safe Space symbol, which features the LGBTQ pride flag and displays a community of triangles that honor the gay pink triangle and lesbian black triangle from Nazi Germany during World War II. These symbols were assigned to and then reclaimed by gay men and lesbians, respectively.[79]

It's amazing how much of our political debate these days revolves around the presence of hidden Nazis, as if Adolf Hitler escaped the destruction of Berlin in 1945 and has been walking amongst us ever since amassing the greatest army in the West. There is something cosmically ironic about a movement reclaiming a symbol of oppression from a tyrannical regime, then adopting an ideology proclaiming which races and classes should have more dominance in society. History doesn't necessarily repeat, but it often seems to rhyme. Uttamchandani continued:

In a society that stigmatizes those who are not in the dominant group, it is important for those that have privilege to act in allyship.

Allyship consists of challenging the multiplicity of oppressive experiences, including racism, genderism, sexism, ableism, etc. that those students experience.[80]

This is the same dichotomy as presented in the concept of "target" and "agent" identities: that the mere existence of a larger group of one people must inevitably result in the domination of the smaller group. And the only way to escape this nightmarish societal system is to gain allies (and accomplices) and overthrow the dominant group. In addition, your educational experience will not be filled with kind people, wiser because they're older than you, trying to help you find your path through life, but only with a "multiplicity of oppressive experiences" designed to keep minorities subservient or dead, while those in the majority are taught to keep the others down.

In the world view of DEI activists, society can never be a collaboration, but must always remain a war between groups over the amount of power they wield.

That world stands in complete opposition to the ideal of universal brotherhood imagined by Dr. Martin Luther King, Jr, and the idea of the American constitutional republic he believed in and fought for.

The next concept the instructors presented was the "Gender Triangle," which was a little confusing, as it had four parts. Wouldn't that make it the "Gender Square"? Maybe it's a self-identified triangle. The four parts were:

> *Body*: How your body exists and changes.
> *Attribution*: How you are perceived by others.
> *Expression*: How you present yourself.
> *Gender Identity*: How you see yourself on the inside.[81]

In fairness to the triangle image, they put "Gender Identity" in the middle of the triangle, along with an image of a brain, suggesting that one's perception is tied to the way others perceive you, how you present yourself, and the physical attributes of one's body. In a sense this isn't completely unreasonable, but it raises more questions. This is the second class to instruct that gender identity resides in the mind, in one's ideal self-perception.

If gender is not connected to biology or one's body, what purpose is served by removing genitalia or issuing hormones to resolve an issue in one's mind?

This is a question, however, that cannot be asked in a "safe space." The problem with safe spaces is that they're created in such a way that all views which challenge the tenants of intersectionality or diversity, equity, and inclusion are forbidden in order to keep the area "safe" for LGBTQIA+ people.

In addition, young people are encouraged to keep what happens in these spaces from their parents.

This cult-like atmosphere in classrooms, or any other area designated as a safe space, continually affirms gender exploration and the transition of those with identity issues, while making the rest of the group activists for LGBTQIA+ and intersectional causes.

Systematically, both students and staff are changed into activists for the LGBTQIA+ ideology under the guise of "safety." Students are not taught to be confident in who they are despite criticism they may receive from others. Instead, the world which these zealous activists intend to create has no criticism; the environment will be made comfortable for anyone deemed marginalized, despite what it may mean for others and in defiance of reality.

There are unavoidable consequences for ignoring reality.

>«

What are the results of all this gender-bending?

In week five of the training, we were presented with this information:

> In 2011, following a rise in suicides of LGBTQ+ youths, California passed the Fair, Accurate, Inclusive, and Respectful (FAIR) Education Act. This gave requirements to schools to have increased representation of LGBTQ+ individuals in history and social science education. As a result, textbook manufacturers were sometimes forced to include or suggest that prominent historical figures were LGBTQ+.[82]

This is a fair account. There was a rise in suicides among LGBTQIA+ youth around 2011. A bit puzzling from an ally's perspective because this was during the years when Barak Obama was the first Black man to be President of the United States twice, and if anything, it would seem to have been a time of greater liberal acceptance. Added to that fact is the question of why this would happen in liberal California, which would be among the most welcoming of all states to gay and transgender lifestyles.

In other words, the problem has been identified, but not its cause. However, DEI and queer activists tell us the solution is to include more LGBTQIA+ individuals in the school textbooks.

Let's subject that claim to a more rigorous analysis. It might be more relevant that young people are more affected by their culture than what they read about in their textbooks. However, the lesson's answer was to lie about certain historical figures as a response to this rise in the suicide rate of LGBTQIA+ youth:

> Similarly, McGraw-Hill initially rejected a request to refer to poet Langston Hughes as gay because, according to the textbook publisher, "there is no definitive evidence or scholarly consensus [that] he was gay (Harrington, 2017). However, in the end, the publisher added that Hughes "was a famous gay African American poet." Supplemental instruction for teachers now also includes LGBTQ+ individuals and issues. For instance, McGraw Hill added the following to a teacher's edition: Though [Walt] Whitman never publicly addressed his sexuality, his poetry, letters, and journals suggest that Whitman would identify as gay if he was alive today... Whitman shared a decades-long romantic friendship with bus conductor Peter Doyle. Though the two never lived together, Doyle was Whitman's muse (Harrington, 2017).[83]

Is this where we are? If you can't find the past you want, you lie about it?

Here's an idea worth considering: Maybe confusing children and adolescents about the sexuality of random adults isn't a good thing. Maybe they're not mature enough to make decisions that will change them for life, such as taking puberty blockers or having surgery. Some days, children and teens will feel one thing, and the next day they feel something else.

Why are we locking them into an identity, when at this time in their life their feelings may be fluid?

They will have the rest of their lives to deal with their sexuality and relationships. Maybe it's a better idea to let these feelings mature before acting to alter them, irreparably, forever.

Perhaps this attempt to make adolescents feel positive about their sexuality falls into the same trap as the well-intentioned "Just Say No" drug prevention program of former First Lady Nancy Reagan. A 2014 article in *Scientific American* detailed why this approach not only failed but may have encouraged the very behavior it sought to curb, focusing on the Drug Abuse Resistance Education (D.A.R.E.) program:

> Despite this fanfare, data indicate that the program does little or nothing to combat substance abuse in youth. A meta-analysis (mathematical review) in 2009 of 20 controlled studies by statisticians Wei Pan, then at the University of Cincinnati, and Haiyan Bai of the University of Central Florida revealed that teens enrolled in the program were just as likely to use drugs as were those who received no intervention....
>
> Worse, D.A.R.E. programs may occasionally backfire when it comes to the use of milder substances, such as alcohol and cigarettes. In a 2002 review psychologist Chudley Werch, now president of "PreventionPLUSWellness" in Jacksonville, Fla., and health educator Deborah Owen of the University of North Florida reported a slight tendency for teens who went through D.A.R.E. to be more likely to drink and smoke than adolescents not exposed to the program.[84]

Conservatives thought it would be a great idea to talk to kids about substance abuse, but reality showed that it didn't make much of a difference and may have made the problem worse.

Perhaps the same is true of progressives who want to talk to kids about their gender identity and sexuality.

Maybe both conservatives and progressives should simply declare kids off limits for any type of ideological advocacy.

It's fine to give them the facts about these issues, maybe even share some of your personal opinions if the parents approve, but after that, let them make their own decisions in the context of who they are and their family situations.

We cannot determine the intent of these advocates outside of what they tell us. Do they seek to help or harm? But their methods seem to indicate that they are comfortable using gradual and subtle techniques to draw students into the DEI ideology in a manner more akin to indoctrination than education.

Despite any possible good intentions, Americans must strongly oppose this effort to expose children to sexual material before they are emotionally and intellectually capable of dealing with it. Children also shouldn't be emotionally manipulated into believing in racial victimization or guilt in their schools or encouraged to be radical activists. While we're at it, maybe convincing young children that they're the opposite sex should be off limits until we determine the cause of the suicides.

Let's not pave the road to hell with these "good" intentions.

4

FOLLOW THE MONEY

You might be curious how all these activists have the resources, reach, and access to infiltrate and influence some of the largest and most influential organizations, such as Hasbro.

The answer is simple: It takes planning and money. Lots of money. You'll probably be shocked by how much planning, and perhaps more important, how *much* money is being directed into these efforts.

Let's examine one of the most influential and well-funded "anti-racist" and "queer affirming" organizations: Black Lives Matter (BLM). According to the Black Lives Matter Global Foundation:

> We see ourselves as part of the global Black family, and we are aware of the different ways we are impacted or privileged as Black people who exist in different parts of the world.
>
> We make space for transgender brothers and sisters to participate and lead.
>
> We disrupt the Western-prescribed nuclear family structure requirement by supporting each other as extended families and "villages" that collectively care

for one another, especially our children, to the degree that mothers, parents, and children are comfortable.

We foster a queer-affirming network. When we gather, we do so with the intention of freeing ourselves from the tight grip of heteronormative thinking, or rather, the belief that all in the world are heterosexual (unless s/he or they disclose otherwise).[85]

An organization that exploded onto the national stage in the wake of the death of George Floyd on May 25, 2020, precipitating a series of riots in the summer of 2020 resulting in more than $1 billion in property damage[86] (primarily in minority areas) and multiple deaths.[87]

Even though BLM is organized under existing laws, it's more accurate to view it like the pirates and buccaneers of the sixteenth and seventeenth centuries, raiding the treasure ships of the Spanish Armada as they plied the Atlantic between Europe, the New World, and the Caribbean.

Unless you're a student of history, you may not realize that for a good portion of time, the pirates and buccaneers were part of the maritime empire of Great Britain, given official sanction by a "letter of marque" from government officials in London. This was done under the reign of Queen Elizabeth I, and some of her favored sea dogs are names known to us today, such as Sir Walter Raleigh and Sir Francis Drake. It's true that pirates could become rich, but they were also the ones taking all the risk to take down the Spanish navy and Spain's commercial vessels. In other words, the pirates were one of the first examples of "state-sponsored terrorism," enabled by humanity's entrepreneurial instincts.

However, when Great Britain made peace with Spain, many of these buccaneers found themselves without a profession—or they hadn't quite reached their financial goals—and decided to continue raiding, often putting themselves in direct conflict with the British navy. (Spoiler alert: the pirates lost.) This may serve as a warning for today's race hustlers and agents of chaos: please be under no illusion that when you cease to be of use to your financial masters, or start to think on your own, they will turn on you with every weapon at their disposal.

No independent thinking will be allowed.

If we're comparing today's activist groups, such as BLM, to the pirates and buccaneers of old, the questions are: Who is Great Britain in this analogy? What is the powerful force allowing this agitation in our society?

The evidence suggests it to be the great non-profit foundations, such as the Tides Foundation, which provide the funds necessary to enable these modern-day buccaneers to cause so much carnage and destruction in the American body politic.

There is a hidden structure beneath what appears to be the anarchy of our current situation. This is how the Tides Foundation is described by the group Influence Watch, which monitors the effect of advocacy groups on legislation:

> The Tides Foundation is a major center-left grantmaking organization and major pass-through funder to numerous left-leaning nonprofits. The San Francisco, California-based 501(c)(3) nonprofit was founded in 1976 by Drummond Pike, a professional political activist who has since retired from the organization, to fund grants from liberal donors to center-left nonprofits using donor advised funds, encouraging individuals to donate to Tides since they would hold an advisory role in its grantmaking. Donor-advised funds are a kind of charitable "savings account" in which donors gift funds to grow in Tides' investment accounts before advising Tides to pay out the funds in grants to other (typically left-leaning) nonprofits.
>
> Since 2007, the Tides Foundation has reported revenues totaling $2.6 billion. In 2020, the Tides Foundation paid out $607 million in grants.[88]

You're probably shaking your head after reading that passage. One can "invest" money with the Tides Foundation, then when the fancy strikes you, "advise" Tides to donate it to the cause of your choice.

In other words, it is a legal way to whitewash the dark money that has become so prevalent in politics. And this particular illiberal organization has been doing it since 1976.

How does this connect to BLM?

We need to talk about a little organization called Thousand Currents.[89] Keeping with the nautical theme, the Tides Foundation has a number of "cut-out" organizations, legal entities that it creates and pretends are independent organizations—a mere façade for murky political fundraising.

How can we determine this to be true?

There are several clues. Both are based in San Francisco, and the address of Thousand Currents is 585 Market Street, home to many other Tides Nexus entities. This is a description of Thousand Currents from Influence Watch:

> Thousand Currents is a left-of-center grantmaking organization that was founded in 1985 as the International Development Exchange and changed its name to Thousand Currents in 2016. Thousand Currents provides funding to activists in developing nations (i.e.: the so-called "global south").
>
> As an example, Thousand Currents, in partnership with Global Greengrants Fund, Grassroots International, and Urgent Action Fund for Women's Human Rights, founded the Climate Leaders in Movement Action Fund (CLIMA). CLIMA is a human rights and environmental mitigation project focused on developing countries. The organization has the goal of raising $10 million between 2018 and 2022.[90]

At first glance, this group might not appear very threatening. After all, who doesn't want human rights and environmental protection in developing countries? This all sounds very laudable. And yet, why was this organization, supposedly dedicated to the developing world, the main partner of BLM from 2016 to 2020? As detailed by Influence Watch:

> In 2016, representatives of the Black Lives Matter (BLM) movement approached Thousand Currents for fiscal management and administrative assistance. This partnership led to a fiscal sponsorship that launched the Black Lives Matter Global Network Foundation. The W.K. Kellogg Foundation provided a three-year grant of $900,000 through Thousand Currents to help organize local BLM chapters. Beginning in 2016, Thousand Currents supported BLM's assistance to protestors at Standing Rock Sioux Reservation who were opposing the use of the Dakota Access oil pipeline. A BLM news release declared the 1,100-mile pipeline through the central United States to be an example of "environmental racism" because a portion of it ran within close proximity to native land.[91]

BLM is interested in oil and Native American rights. And the organization uses Thousand Currents, a group in San Francisco, to run things. But what happens when George Floyd is killed, and donations start pouring in, and Thousand Currents can't handle the extra work?

Who does Thousand Currents go running to for reinforcement? The Tides Foundation. Here's the Tides Foundation press release from July 2, 2020, announcing the new collaboration:

> Tides welcomes Black Lives Matter as a new partner.

> Tides Foundation has launched the Black Lives Matter Support Fund, which will support BLM's grantmaking activities. This unique partnership will further amplify the extraordinary, unparalleled suc-

cess of BLM's chapter led, decentralized organizational model, while also allowing BLM to build the necessary infrastructure for sustainability.

BLM formalized its relationship with Tides Foundation, after BLM's prior fiscal sponsor, Thousand Currents, made the strategic decision to sunset fiscal sponsorships in order to focus on its core grantmaking work. BLM is creating impactful, historic social change, not only in the US but throughout the world, and Tides is proud to be their partner.[92]

Notice how BLM is organized to have maximum flexibility to cause societal harm, while avoiding legal responsibility. The press release praises the organization's "decentralized organizational model."

The same strategy used by Al Qaeda, Russian hackers given sanction by Moscow's Putin regime, and unfortunately, our own intelligence services. It's how you can set things in motion, like a big rock rolling down a hill, and evade liability when it demolishes somebody's house.

The Capital Research Center (CRC), the parent organization of Influence Watch, took a look at these activities in a July 28, 2020, article and noted the following:

The Tides Center specializes in "incubation," using its 501(c)(3) tax-exempt status as a shield sheltering countless activist groups while they wait to receive their own tax-exempt statuses from the IRS. One Tides spinoff is People for the American Way, infamous for its 1987 smear campaign that blocked the confirmation of Judge Robert Bork to the Supreme Court and for protesting the confirmation of Justice Brett Kavanaugh in 2018.

The Tides Center itself is a branch of the larger Tides Foundation, a pass-through funder and pillar of the modern activist Left. Tides was conceived in the mid-1970s as an innovative pass-through—effectively a middleman for liberal donors angling to anonymously support left-wing causes. Donors cut checks to Tides, which manages their finances in individual "savings accounts" (called donor-advised funds) until the donors indicate a final recipient for the funds. Their funds are then paid out as Tides grants, masking the original benefactors' identities from public scrutiny.[93]

Although every part of this scheme is likely to be legal (or the IRS averts its gaze from any possible criminality), it should be deeply troubling to every American. How can one possibly tell which organizations are led by genuine activists, and which are simply paid left-wing fronts?

How do we know who is donating to the Tides Foundation? In many cases we may not know, and that is the point. But sometimes we get clues, even hard evidence, that Tides employs known and convicted terrorists. According to the CRC:

> While in many cases donors cannot be identified, six-and-seven-figure grant totals to Thousand Currents earmarked for BLM Global Network Foundation have been traced to a number of liberal foundations, including the NoVo Foundation, W.K. Kellogg Foundation, and Borealis Philanthropy.
>
> CRC also revealed that Thousand Currents' board of directors included Susan Rosenberg, a former member of the communist Weather Underground—which planted bombs across the United States—and convicted domestic terrorist who served a 16-year sentence in federal prison for possession of 740 pounds of unstable dynamite stolen from a Texas construction firm in 1980.

> Rosenberg was described as a "human and prisoner rights advocate" on Thousand Currents' website. Thousand Currents removed the webpage (archived) for its board shortly after CRC published Rosenberg's connection to armed violence and terrorism.[94]

Consider the case of Susan Rosenberg, convicted domestic terrorist, placed on the board of directors of the Tides Foundation—possibly the most important of any of the left-wing foundations. Imagine if a similarly prominent conservative organization, say the Federalist Society or the Proud Boys, put on its board a member of some radical right-wing militia. The mainstream media would *never* stop talking about it. But Susan Rosenberg, the dynamite lady, went quietly into the night.

However, this wasn't a purge of the undesirable elements. It was simply window dressing. These domestic terrorists continued using the immense financial resources of these charitable organizations to bring about the change that their bombs never could.

>«

How difficult is it to radicalize people?

We're raised to believe that a big betrayal can only be brought about by the promise of enormous riches and power, like the devil whisking Jesus to the highest mountaintop and tempting Him with the entire world if He would abandon God.

The truth is that betrayal is mostly an inside job, spurred along by small rewards—a little betrayal here and there—until the soul has been corrupted, as American soldiers captured by the Chinese discovered during the Korean War.

At the time it happened it was a shock to the American psyche. As one former *New York Times* bureau chief wrote in his book about those times:

> Americans should have been able to celebrate the release of 7,200 soldiers from communist prisons

after an armistice ended the fighting in Korea in July 1953. Instead, they recoiled in shock. Many prisoners, it turned out, had written statements criticizing the United States or praising communism. Some had confessed to committing war crimes. Twenty-one chose to stay behind in North Korea or China. The Pentagon announced they were considered deserters and would be executed if found.

Most astonishing of all, several pilots among the released prisoners asserted that they had dropped bioweapons from their warplanes—contradicting Washington's fierce insistence that it had never deployed such weapons. "The most used germ bomb was a 500-pounder," one pilot reported. "Each had several compartments to hold different kinds of germs. Insects like fleas and spiders were kept separate from rats and voles."[95]

How had these Americans turned against their country and embraced their communist foe? What happened to those Americans in these prisoner of war camps? Surprisingly, the American soldiers were generally well fed and cared for—it was the psychological breakdown of these men that proved most effective.

In the late 1950s, a psychologist named Robert Jay Lifton studied the former inmates of these Chinese and Korean prisoner of war camps to determine what had made them turn traitor, or in the common parlance of the time, become "brainwashed."[96]

What is truly terrifying is how simple these techniques can be, which usually involve three distinct stages: first, breaking down the self; second, introducing the possibility of salvation; and third, rebuilding the self. In the North Korean and Chinese camps, when the communists got the American soldiers to inform on each other for small violations, they rarely even bothered with punishing the offending soldier. Instead, they simply let the soldier know who had informed on him, then put the two soldiers back together in the same unit. It destroyed the morale of the unit, creating a sense of isolation, and is often credited with being the reason for the high rate of suicide among captured American soldiers.

Determine for yourself if these foundations and the organizations which they support are in essence doing the same thing. As detailed by How Stuff Works, breaking down the self usually involves four specific steps:

> **Assault on identity: You are not who you think you are.** This is a systematic attack on a target's sense of self (also called his identity or ego) and his core belief system. The agent denies everything that makes the target who he is...

> **Guilt: You are bad.** While the identity crisis is setting in, the agent is simultaneously creating an overwhelming sense of guilt in the target. He repeatedly and mercilessly attacks the subject for any "sin" the target has committed, large or small...

> **Self-betrayal: Agree with me that you are bad.** Once the subject is disoriented and drowning in guilt, the agent forces him (either with the threat of physical harm or continuance of the mental attack) to denounce his family, friends and peers who share the same "wrong" belief system that he holds...

> **Breaking point: Who am I, where am I and what am I supposed to do?** With his identity in crisis, experiencing deep shame and having betrayed what he has always believed in, the target may undergo what in the lay community is referred to as a "nervous breakdown."[97]

You could be a renowned civil rights activist de-escalating racial tensions, yet today's progressive activists are ready to convince you that you are protecting your "White privilege" by insisting on hard work and competence. It seems that the modern progressive Left is working overtime to make you feel bad about yourself. Not satisfied with being racist? You're also probably transphobic, an insurrection-ist against the Constitution and want the earth to die from climate change (although the conservatives, libertarians, and displaced liber-als I've met are all constitutionalists).

Politicians and activists used to challenge the public to live up to their highest ideals, but much of what passes for media discussion is one side (not always, but usually, the Left) claiming that the other side consists of terrible people.

This does not bring a community together, but tears it apart, which is just the thing those in power want because it makes the cit-izens easier to control: simple "divide and conquer."

If you imagine that we're all in an open-air Chinese re-education camp, dedicated to breaking the bonds that keep any group together, then much of today's chaos makes more sense. Like a prisoner under-going torture, we simply want it to stop.

That's when the promise of salvation is offered, and many are willing to take it:

> First, the brainwasher shows leniency. With the target in a state of crisis, the agent offers some small kind-ness or reprieve from the abuse...

> Next, the brainwasher offers an opportunity for con-fession. For the first time in the brainwashing process, the target is faced with the contrast between the guilt and pain of identity assault and the sudden relief of leniency. The target may feel a desire to reciprocate the kindness offered to him, and at that point, the agent may present the possibility of confession as a means to relieving guilt and pain...

> Next, releasing the guilt is a key step. The embattled target is relieved to learn there is an external cause of wrongness, that it is not he himself who is inescap-

ably bad—this means he can escape his wrongness by escaping the wrong belief system. All he has to do is denounce the people and institutions associated with that belief system, and he won't be in pain anymore.[98]

It's a diabolically clever strategy for breaking the will of the enemy that does not rely on physical abuse, deprivation, or what we commonly think of as torture. There are no cattle prods, waterboarding, threats of immediate execution, or bamboo slivers shoved under the fingernails to achieve the desired result.

> The final stage is called "Rebuilding the Self," to complete the process. The subject is then presented with a path to alleged progress and harmony. In other words, "If you want, you can choose good." At this stage, the agent stops the abuse, offering the target physical comfort and mental calm in conjunction with the new belief system. The target is made to feel that it is he who must choose between the old and the new, giving the target the sense that his fate is in his own hands.... The choice is not a difficult one. The new identity is safe and desirable because it is nothing like the one that led to his breakdown.[99]

This doesn't seem much different from the strategy used by many activist groups that want people to "confess" their White privilege.

It seems that most, if not all, of the population genuinely wants racial equality. What we should then expect from organizations that claim that we haven't made enough progress is a clear series of steps to achieve their desired result.

However, when one looks at the history of organizations of this type, such as BLM, it seems a different agenda is at play.

Is this because the foundations that support Black Lives Matter are getting exactly what they want?

»«

In order to accurately describe the history of BLM, it's probably best that we look to news organizations outside the US, such as the BBC, in order to get a clearer perspective. As the BBC described the use of the slogan "Black Lives Matter" and the subsequent creation of the BLM organization in 2021:

> The slogan was widely used after the death of Trayvon Martin in Florida, in 2012. The unarmed black 17-year-old was shot by neighborhood watch volunteer George Zimmerman.
>
> Support grew following other police killings, including Eric Garner, who died in a chokehold, and Michael Brown, who was killed by an officer who said he acted in self-defense.
>
> In the summer of 2020 George Floyd, an unarmed black man, was murdered by a police officer who knelt on his neck.
>
> Protests using the #BLM slogan took place worldwide and the hashtag #BlackLivesMatter was used tens of millions of times.[100]

What you have are four high-profile deaths of Black men. Let's look at each one individually.

George Zimmerman was acquitted in the death of Trayvon Martin when it was proven to the jury's satisfaction that Zimmerman acted in self-defense.[101]

After a long investigation by Justice Department officials into the death of Eric Garner, it was decided not to bring federal civil rights charges or state charges against the officer.[102] However, Garner's death did ignite a nationwide debate about police chokeholds in response to relatively minor crimes such as, in this instance, selling cigarettes illegally. The officer in question, Daniel Pantaleo, was fired without a pension after it became clear that he had used an illegal chokehold in the arrest.[103]

The Michael Brown shooting in Ferguson, Missouri, in 2014 was the subject of multiple investigations. As reported by the *New York Times*:

> Six years after a white police officer shot and killed Michael Brown, a Black teenager in Ferguson, Mo., another investigation has come to the same conclusion as the first: The officer should not be charged.
>
> The officer, Darren Wilson, already had been cleared by a grand jury and a federal investigation [by the Obama Department of Justice] months after the shooting in 2014. But Thursday's announcement by a new prosecutor, Wesley Bell, most likely marks the end of the legal saga in a case that started the global rise of the Black Lives Matter movement, which has led to some major shifts in American policing and forced a renewed conversation about racism.[104]

Think of what six years of investigation would do to your life. That's what officer Darren Wilson went through. But even Obama's justice department found that there wasn't enough information to bring charges. Can we stop talking about Michael Brown, who was a known thug? Oh, and by the way, he never said, "Hands up, don't shoot!"[105] That was in the report from the Obama justice department as well.

Which leaves us with the case of George Floyd, admittedly a difficult case. On one side there is the evidence that Floyd was a felon, previously convicted of armed robbery in the state of Texas with a history of violence:

> An attorney for one of four former Minneapolis officers charged in George Floyd's death is highlighting

Floyd's past crimes and history of drug abuse, calling him an ex-con and "evident danger to the community." Another is seizing on Floyd's medical issues and addiction, saying he likely died from fentanyl, and not a knee on his neck.[106]

George Floyd was not anybody's image of a model citizen. And the initial part of the interaction with officers was not the way a typical citizen responds to police officers:

Body-camera footage from the day Floyd died shows [police officers Thomas] Lane and [Alex] Kueng approaching a panicked Floyd, who says, "I'm not a bad guy!" and struggles, begging not to be put in a squad car. Gray wrote that the video shows Floyd had something in his mouth that looked like a fentanyl pill, which disappeared. Autopsy reports show Floyd had fentanyl in his system.

Gray and Eric Nelson, Chauvin's attorney, wrote that during a May 2019 arrest, Floyd wouldn't listen to officers' commands, put something in his mouth, had to be physically removed from a vehicle, then began to cry. In that case, several opioid pills were found, along with cocaine, they wrote.[107]

That gives you some idea of the character of George Floyd. This is not to poison the well, but present both sides of what occurred. Floyd was not a typical law-abiding citizen, although the open question is how he appeared to the officers on that fateful day in Minneapolis.

On May 25, 2020, while attempting to subdue Floyd, officer Derek Chauvin pressed his knee against Floyd's neck and back for eight to nine minutes, possibly suffocating him. This is the sentence that officer Chauvin received for his actions:

> Former Minneapolis police officer Derek Chauvin has been sentenced to more than 20 years in prison for violating George Floyd's civil rights.
>
> Chauvin pleaded guilty to the separate federal civil rights charges in December.
>
> He is already serving a 22-year state prison sentence for the on-duty murder of Mr. Floyd, a 46-year-old black man.
>
> The two sentences will run concurrently, and Chauvin will now be moved to a federal prison.[108]

Was excessive force used against George Floyd? According to reports, Chauvin was entitled to use *more* force (such as a taser) than he chose with the restraint.[109] That's what the justice system found, the same system that freed George Zimmerman in the Trayvon Martin case and officer Darren Wilson in the Michael Brown case.

I think we can all agree that some police interactions do not occur, and some police officers do not perform their duties, in a way we would expect. When those situations take place, the officers should be prosecuted to the full extent of the law.

The question then becomes, how do groups like BLM respond to these incidents? Do they suggest helpful steps, or do they use such tragedies to fit a predetermined narrative? Writes the BBC:

> Some people argue that using the term Black Lives Matter demonstrates support for an organization of the same name. It was started in 2013 by three black women: Alicia Garza, Patrisse Cullors, and Opal Tometi.
>
> Among its main goals are stopping police brutality and fighting for courts to treat black people equally. Its demands for equality also include mental health, the LGBT community and voting rights.

However, former US secretary of housing and developments [sic], Ben Carson, said people with noble aims had been taken advantage of by a "Marxist-driven organization" that supports "taking down the model of a Western family structures."

Carol Swain, a political commentator and former professor, said: "[BLM is] using black people to advance a Marxist agenda."

Replying to critics, Patrice Cullors said "I do believe in Marxism," but added: "I'm working on making sure people don't suffer."[110]

Have we found our answer? BLM is using Black people to advance a Marxist agenda. The words of Patrisse Cullors are a confession that she is doing exactly that. Even Marx, Engels, and Stalin would have said that they were pursuing their aims so that "people don't suffer."

But it's too simplistic to paint this clash as one between Black communists and White capitalists. It smacks of a false narrative, designed to conceal the plans of actors who remain hidden just off-stage.

A more sinister game is afoot, one that the pirates and buccaneers of these left-wing organizations would do well to understand, lest they find themselves bereft of support, as the pirates of the 16th century did when England signed a peace treaty with Spain and turned the full force of its military force on annihilating its former allies.

>«

The Tides Foundation advertises itself as an American public charity and financial sponsor, working to advance progressive causes and policy initiatives in areas such as the environment, healthcare, labor issues, immigrant rights, LGBTQIA+ rights, women's rights, and human rights.

In its simplest form, the Tides Foundation distributes money from anonymous donors to other organizations, which are often, if not exclusively, progressive.

In other words, the Tides Foundation launders money to activist groups from individuals who want to keep their identities secret. It allows the Tides Foundation to claim plausible deniability that it is funding political violence.

How much money are we talking about?

In 2020, the Tides Foundation listed its annual revenue as $511 million.

That is $511,000,000—*$511 million* in annual revenue.

The Tides Foundation organizational makeup consists of four main funds: the Advocacy Fund, the Tides Foundation, the Wikimedia Foundation (which manages Wikipedia), and Tides Advocacy.

It probably won't come as much of a shock to learn that the members of the boards of directors of these various entities circulate among the various foundations like a cabal of corporate fat cats. It's all a big progressive party and they pretend to care about the little guy, but when the mom-and-pop stores shut down (as they did during the COVID-19 pandemic, or when American inner cities burned), where do residents go for their needs?

They often have little choice but to visit big-time retailers and online stores owned by the billionaire class.

Pretending to care about the poor and line their pockets with record profits in the process—it's a pretty good hustle.

And how well do these charitable foundations work with each other? It takes a lot of grants to reach $511 million.

Here's a partial list of some of the largest financial contributors to the Tides Foundation:

There's the Annie E. Casey Foundation, which is "devoted to developing a brighter future for millions of children and young people with respect to their educational, economic, social, and health outcomes."[111] From 2014 to 2016, the Annie E. Casey Foundation donated $4,965,186 to Tides organizations.[112]

Then there's the Accountable Justice Action Fund, which states on its website: "The Accountable Justice Action Fund supports criminal justice reform, with a focus on reforming prosecution and equipping local and national groups to increase accountability in prosecutorial elections."[113]

Since 2019, the Accountable Justice Action Fund has awarded eleven individual grants totaling $4,222,142 to the Tides Advocacy Fund.[114]

The Bauman Family Foundation states that: "Since its inception, the Foundation has supported environmental health, toxics right to know, open government, and civic participation. It has also made special grants in health care and the arts."[115] (You get the idea. After a while all these foundations start to sound the same. Justice, equity, save the planet, defend the children, defeat the evil Republicans.)

The Bauman Family Foundation reports that it gave $18,780,000 to the Tides Foundation From 2011 to 2020.[116]

The Bill and Melinda Gates Foundation - $26,809,905 to the Tides Nexus entities since the year 2000.[117]

The Carnegie Corporation of New York - $3,552,100 to Tides Nexus entities since 2005.[118]

The David and Lucile Packard Foundation - $10,171,072 to Tides Nexus entities since 2017.[119]

The Ford Foundation - $102,798,731 to Tides Nexus entities since 2007.[120]

The George Soros Foundation to Promote Open Society - $31,574,380 to Tides Nexus entities since 2016.[121]

The Jennifer and Jonathan Allan Soros Foundation - $4,887,438 to Tides Nexus entities since 2011.[122]

The Gill Foundations, a collection of lesbian, gay, bisexual, and transgender equal rights groups (administered by the Tides Foundation), has reported donations of $3,292,700 to Tides Nexus entities since 2006.[123]

The John D. and Catherine T. MacArthur Foundation - $17,010,102 to Tides Nexus entities since 1987.[124]

The Nick and Leslie Hanauer Foundation - $640,384 to Tides Nexus entities since 2001.[125]

The Oak Foundation USA - $6,000,000 to Tides Nexus entities since 2019.[126]

The Omidyar Network Fund - $2,566,104 to Tides Nexus entities since entities since 2017.[127]

The Robert Wood Johnson Foundation - $29,261,281 to Tides Nexus entities since 1993.[128]

The Rockefeller Brothers Fund - $6,325,000 to Tides Nexus entities since 2017.[129]

The Rockefeller Family Fund - $460,914 in Tides Nexus entities since 2003.[130]

The Rockefeller Philanthropy Advisors - $3,525,000 to Tides Nexus entities since 2001.[131]

The W.R. Kellogg Foundation - $60,829,942 to Tides Nexus entities since 1991.[132]

The Wallace Global Fund II - $8,621,001 to Tides Nexus entities from 2008 to 2016.[133]

The William and Flora Hewlett - $51,758,408 to Tides Nexus entities since 2014.[134]

In 2016, the Google Foundation - $59,000,000 to Tides Nexus entities.[135]

This information, representing more than $400 million from the largest corporations on the planet, represent an ocean of money on which these left-wing, Marxism-inspired organizations can sail.

The question is, why are a bunch of capitalists giving money to Marxist organizations?

Perhaps they have a death wish?

Or is there another, more plausible, agenda at play—one in which the richest people on the planet make even larger profits at the expense of the largely unknowing average citizen?

>«

In the interest of fairness, let's look at the "defund the police" movement led by BLM. This is directly from the Defund the Police website, maintained by BLM, accessed on October 4, 2022. The site lists five main objections to policing: (1) Traffic Services, (2) Violent Crime, (3) Gender-Based Violence, (4) Investigative Services, and

(5) Bylaw Enforcement, Parking, and Minor Services. Let's examine each one of these in turn:

Traffic Services

> One of the services that police regularly provide are traffic services. But again, here is an area where armed, uniformed police are unnecessary. Where police are engaging in traffic services, their intervention could result in more harm to other vehicles using the road. When a UPS truck was stolen in Florida during the course of a robbery in which no one was harmed, the police prioritized the recovery of the (likely insured) jewelry and capture of the robber over the safety of everyone else on the road. Several police cars engaged in a high-speed chase, crashing into other vehicles on the road. Eventually, police exited their vehicles and began an outrageous shooting spree. Multiple innocent bystanders were killed in the process.
>
> Beyond situations like the horrific example above, police are more likely to stop Black people for supposed traffic "infractions," when no one's safety is at risk. What is the purpose of these stops? Oftentimes, a mere request to justify a traffic stop from a Black driver can result in the type of escalation that culminates in death, like Sandra Bland.[136]

If one takes the position that this approach is a genuine attempt to address aggressive policing, it is true that cops have been over-incentivized to act zealously in traffic stops, to the detriment of everyone.

Probably the best-informed analysis of the problem of aggressive policing in general was covered in the magnificent book *Talking with Strangers: What We Should Know About the People We Don't Know* by Malcolm Gladwell. Gladwell had been troubled by the Sandra Bland case, in which a young Black woman, new to Prairie View, Texas, had just interviewed for a job at a radio station. She was pulled over by a local policeman, Brian Encinia, an unnecessary argument developed between the two, she was arrested and jailed, and then hung herself two days later in the jail.

Gladwell argues that the Sandra Bland case was the tragic result of bad decisions by police departments across the country, creating ineffective policies which often result in tragic outcomes. Specifically, taking advantage of Supreme Court decisions that found less of an expectation of privacy in private vehicles than in private residences, police officers were encouraged to go "beyond the ticket" to rattle drivers in the hope of revealing those who were engaged in criminal activity.

The roots of these policies were established in the early 1990s in a series of policing experiments in Kansas City. After finding that added patrols and gun-buyback programs didn't decrease crime, the government decided to use aggressive traffic enforcement in a crime-ridden area known as District 144, which comprised 0.64 square miles—a few city blocks. Gladwell detailed the instructions given to these officers in this extremely small high-crime area:

> They were freed from all other law enforcement obligations. They didn't have to answer radio calls or rush to accident scenes. Their instructions were clear: watch out for what you think are suspicious-looking drivers. Use whatever pretext you can find in the traffic code to pull them over. If you're still suspicious, search the car and confiscate any weapon you find. The officers worked every night from 7 p.m. to 1 a.m., seven days a week, for 200 days. And what happened? Outside District 144, where police business was conducted as usual, crime remained as bad as ever. But inside 144? All of the new focused police work cut gun crimes—shootings, murders, woundings—in *half*.[137]

Due to a small crime-ridden area of 0.64 miles, police departments across the country decided that they needed to turn the entire country into District 144, with police instructed to be suspicious of everybody they encountered.

This was exactly the approach that Brian Encinia had taken with Sandra Bland, racing up behind her in his police car, and when she quickly moved over into another lane to allow him to pass, he stopped her for failing to use her turn signal. These tactics, and others, created hostility in the public, as they incentivized police to treat all traffic stops as involving potential criminals. In essence, police were instructed to act like jerks to the citizens they encountered, and then to consider those who complained or appeared rattled as suspects. In North Carolina this approach resulted in a doubling of traffic stops. As recounted by Gladwell:

> Think back to the dramatic increase in traffic stops by the North Carolina State Highway Patrol. In seven years they [sic] went from 400,000 to 800,000. Now, is that because in that time period the motorists of North Carolina suddenly started running more red lights, drinking more heavily and breaking the speed limit more often? Of course not. It's because the state police changed their tactics. They started doing more haystack searches. They instructed their police officers to disregard their natural inclination to default to truth—and start imagining the worst: that young women coming from job interviews might be armed or dangerous, or young men cooling off after a pickup game might be pedophiles.
>
> How many extra guns and drugs did the North Carolina Highway Patrol find with those 400,000 searches? Seventeen. Is it really worth alienating and stigmatizing 399,983 Mikes and Sandras in order to find 17 bad apples?[138]

None of us is well-served by emotional reactions that aren't backed up by facts. The simple truth seems to be that well-intentioned actions to lower crime rates have spun out of control, creating a larger problem than existed in the first place: 400,000 additional traffic stops in North Carolina resulted in seventeen additional arrests and 399,983 citizens asking themselves, "What the hell was all that about?" And this approach has been taken across the country. No wonder people are upset about police behavior.

Malcolm Gladwell is an underappreciated intellectual treasure. Why is there no candidate somewhere running for Congress or the Senate who declares, "On any complex issue, I'm simply going to ask Malcolm Gladwell what he would do." *Talking to Strangers*, is essentially an investigation of what happened to Sandra Bland in her encounter with officer Brian Encinia. As Gladwell writes at the end of the book:

> I said at the beginning of this book that I was not willing to put the death of Sandra Bland aside. I have now watched the videotape of her encounter with Brian Encinia more times that I can count—and each time I do, I become angrier and angrier over the way the case was "resolved." It was turned into something much smaller than it really was: a bad police officer and an aggrieved young black woman. That's not what it was. What went wrong that day on FM 1098 in Prairie View, Texas, was a collective failure. Someone wrote a training manual that foolishly encouraged Brian Encinia to suspect everyone, and he took it to heart. Somebody else higher up in the chain of command at the Texas Highway Patrol misread the evidence and thought it was a good idea to have him and his colleagues conduct Kansas City stops in a low-crime neighborhood. Everyone in his world acted on the presumption that the motorists driving up and down the streets of their corner of Texas could be identified and categorized on the basis

of the tone of their voice, fidgety movements, and fast-food wrappers.[139]

We can see that the "stop and frisk" strategy, as well as other more aggressive policing strategies, started out well-intentioned, and in the appropriate situations (a relatively small high-crime area) they can be highly effective. But by using such aggressive methods in larger areas, the net effect is negative, both in perceptions of the general public and among the poorer members of our society, who in effect become ATMs for local police departments.

BLM is right that current traffic policies need to be revamped—but not that traffic services by local police departments need to be completely abolished.

>«

The next reason why BLM's Defund the Police website argues that police departments should be defunded is because the police do not deter violent crime. This is part of the argument:

Violent Crime

One common refrain in opposition to defunding the police assumes that our society will not be able to effectively respond to violent crime. But we have to remember that police do not prevent violence. In most incidents of violent crime, police are responding to a crime that has already taken place. When this happens, what we need from police is a service that will investigate the crime, and perhaps prevent such crimes from occurring in the future.

Policing is ill-equipped to suit these needs. When victims are not the right kind of victims, police have utterly failed, and at times refused to take the threat seriously. Why would we rely on an institution that has consistently proven that it is rife with systematic anti-Blackness and other forms of discrimination that result in certain communities being deemed unworthy of support? Instead of relying on police, we could rely on investigators from other sectors to carry out investigations. Social workers, sociologists, forensic scientists, doctors, researchers, and other well-trained individuals to fulfill our needs when violent crimes take place.[140]

There is much merit to that argument, even though I do not agree with the conclusion. First, it is true that the police are generally responding to violent crime, rather than preventing it. However, what is not addressed is the extent to which the presence of police deters crime, a phenomenon that can be observed in major cities across the USA.

Only a year after the rallying cry of "defund the police" swept across the country in 2020, cities like New York City and Oakland, California were forced to reinvest in their police after a spike in violent crime.[141] While other cities such as Portland, Oregon; Seattle, Washington; and San Francisco, California continue to decay, as businesses and residents flee the rising crime and the policies that shackle law enforcement.[142] [143]

Similarly, people are likely to have strongly divergent views on whether the police have "utterly failed" in many instances, as well as whether the system is "rife with systematic anti-Blackness."

Maybe it is time for a different approach.

Could the work of police investigation be done by "social workers, sociologists, forensic scientists, doctors, researchers, and other well-trained individuals?" Maybe. We should always be open to innovation. Perhaps this should be tried on a small scale and see how it works out.

Perhaps the threat of police violence against criminals deters a great deal of crime.

>»«

The next BLM argument for defunding the police is based on the problem of gender-based violence. The organization claims:

Gender-Based Violence

> Some skeptics respond to calls to defund the police with concern for people at high risk for gender-based violence. The fear is that society will not be able to protect people against sexual assault and domestic violence. But as a society, we are currently failing to protect people from gender-based violence.

> A woman is killed by a partner in Canada every six days. In the United States, four women are killed by their partners every day. In the US, only 20 percent of all sexual assaults are reported. In Canada, less than ten percent of all sexual assaults are reported to police. National statistics bodies do not collect the same sort of data for trans communities, though there is no doubt that trans people are targeted for violence due to transphobia across North America, with Black women comprising the majority of homicide victims.[144]

This excerpt asserts quite a few dramatic claims. The website goes on to argue that since the police are not good at stopping violence against women, money should be taken from the police and spent on those services that would lower violence against women and transgender individuals. BLM does not clarify that the 80 percent statistic of non-reporting of sexual assault refers to college campuses, using a survey that broadened the definition of "sexual assault" to include "sex under the influence of drugs or alcohol"[145] even in the absence of any coercion. Asserting in addition that there is a similar outbreak of violence against transgender people, and that this is due to rampant "transphobia," without evidence, gives a clear view of the ideological goal.

There is a point to be made that violence against anyone outside of self-defense is a problem. Also, if all women were given .22 revolvers and instructed how to use them, what would be the effect on the sexual crime rate?

»«

The next argument by BLM is about investigation services:

Investigation Services

Police are meant to provide investigation services for us in the event that we experience a theft or burglary or a similar crime. We are inundated with television shows that tell us that police provide expert detective services to bring perpetrators of these kinds of crimes to justice. But these stories are myths and an unjust way to think about the risks that people take when they are living in precarious conditions.

In the United States the clearance rates 2018 for motor-vehicle theft and burglary were less than 15 percent. For theft and property crime, the clearance rates were less than 20 percent. For robbery, the clearance rate was just over 30 percent and for arson, the clearance rate was less than 25 percent....

If we were to defund the police, we could create new investigative services where diverse teams of researchers and investigators, with a mix of scientific, public health and sociological expertise are able to attend to our investigative needs without the inherent anti-Blackness with which the police services approach our unsolved cases.[146]

One can appreciate the facts that BLM lists on clearance rates. What is less certain is which mix of resources and personnel would improve those numbers.

Does BLM realize that there are police officers of all races, ethnicities, sexualities, and both sexes currently in employ across the nation? The mere addition of racial minorities, women, or LGBTQIA+ individuals is once again implied to be a snake-oil remedy for all issues without any evidence to support the claim. On the contrary, defunding the police would leave fewer resources for solving these crime cases.

>«

The final argument on the Defund the Police website is about the failure of police in bylaw enforcement, parking, and minor services.

Bylaw Enforcement, Parking & Minor Services

Across North America, police services attend to minor bylaw enforcement, parking, and minor services like serving warrants. There is no reason for police officers to attend to these services. Minor ticketed offenses and serving warrants for arrests and searches can be delivered by civilian services rather than armed, uniformed officers...

Funding the provision of safe warm places to sleep—that is, meaningfully addressing the housing shortage and homelessness crisis in our cities—offers far more safety than police harassment, ticketing, and criminalization.[147]

BLM does not seem to treat these services with the same racist undertones as some of the other police functions, although it does note that these actions serve to criminalize poverty, a point made by many other commentators. In essence, BLM appears to think of these as unnecessary police services, and that the money would be better spent on other endeavors.

Many will differ with this opinion, but there was little good data for the position of either side. That is, until the success of the BLM agenda in Minneapolis after the death of George Floyd in 2020. In September 2022, CNN examined the city's crime rate in the two years since the BLM agenda was adopted. Despite the problems with policing, the "defund the police" movement seems to be endangering more minority lives and property.

The 2022 CNN examination of the consequences of the "defund the police" movement in Minneapolis, is titled "Once Nicknamed 'Murderapolis,' the City that Became the Center of the 'Defund the Police' Movement is Grappling with Heightened Violent Crime."[148] It reads:

> After the police killing of George Floyd in May of 2020, Minneapolis became a worldwide symbol of the police brutality long endured by Black people. In a kind of Newtonian response, the city became the epicenter of the culturally seismic "Defund the Police" movement....
>
> Now, with its police department under investigation by the Department of Justice, the city of 425,000 is trying to find a way forward amid a period of heightened crime that began shortly after Floyd's death.
>
> That year, the number of murders soared to nearly 80—dwarfing the 2019 body count of 46. It has cooled somewhat this year, though the amount of killing—and violent crime in general—remain elevated far above 2019 levels and homicides are on pace to surpass the 2020 figure.[149]

Facts can be stubborn things. What followed in the wake of the George Floyd protests was an increase in homicides and violent crimes. If we claim to care about "Black lives" we must address this situation. It was not the police who went on a slaughtering spree across Minneapolis—and many other American cities.

To its credit, CNN interviewed Minneapolis residents to get their perspective. K.C. Wilson, a longtime resident of the Twin Cities, said that police withdrew from violent neighborhoods in the aftermath of Floyd's killing, which emboldened criminals—a common sentiment among locals.

> "The criminals were celebrating. They were getting rich," he said. "They were selling drugs openly."

> ...Citing sinking morale in the wake of Floyd's killing, leaders of the Minneapolis Police Department say the officer head count has shrunk from 900 in early 2020 to about 560 in August—a loss of more than a third of the force.[150]

CNN performed a great public service by examining and publicizing the results of the "defund the police" movement. Criminals were emboldened and police were demoralized. The casualties were the members of the poorest communities. These were the comments of Sgt. Betsy Bratner Smith of the National Police Association:

> It's no secret that law enforcement...especially in the last two and a half years, has been badly vilified and wrongly vilified," she told CNN. "You can't call an entire profession racist and expect people to just sit back and say, okay, you know, keep piling on."

> In June, the embattled Minneapolis department was hit with more bad press—this time for its abysmal numbers on unsolved murders in recent years.

> Since 2016, the clearance rate (or the percentage of homicide cases closed) in Minneapolis sank from around 54%—the most recent national average—to 38% in 2020, according to the latest available data from the FBI.[151]

It would appear that the BLM movement has made everything more difficult for the urban poor, and not even CNN could lie about it any further.

But the blame doesn't only rest with BLM—it also rests with the foundations that support it.

Are we supposed to believe that the wealthiest people in America are funding Marxist organizations because they are unaware of what they're paying for? If they're not assumed to be incompetent, then another answer must be more likely.

Is it perhaps that these billionaires are more interested in destroying the free market, preventing the poor from having a path to the middle class, while at the same time convincing the activists that their destruction is but a prelude to a better world?

There are only two possible solutions: (1) These billionaires are stupid, kindling a communist fire that could only burn them to the ground by sheer accident, or (2) they know exactly what they are doing.

I do not believe that these billionaires, or the foundations they support, are stupid. I believe that they know exactly what they are doing.

The destruction of the inner city—and the small businesses that might revitalize them—were always part of the plan of those with the $511 million receipt.

5

CASUALTIES OF THE WAR ON CULTURE

*Why should your right to freedom of speech trump
a trans-person's right "not to be offended"?*

—Cathy Newman, UK Channel 4 news presenter

*Because, in order to be able to think,
you have to risk being offensive.*

—Jordan B. Peterson[152]

From the workplace to the schoolhouse, one of the most proclaimed goals of creating "inclusive" or "safe" spaces is to create an environment where people—particularly marginalized identity groups—receive validation and promotion, free from criticism or judgment. Those with "agent" identities or privileged group status should risk or abdicate their positions to support and ally or become accomplices for "target" identity groups.

These safe spaces, despite the name, are openly hostile spaces to most people. In order to be welcomed into a safe space, it is a prerequisite that one already believe in the validity of "intersectionality" and the value of "inclusion." The stated purpose of a safe space is to validate all non-traditional identity groups and labels, making them "safe" from criticism or "hatred." The mere act of questioning how an obscure identity came to be (the "gender-blender" identity for example) is often enough to get the speaker accused of bigotry or invalidation of a person's existence, and in some extreme cases, is considered tantamount to physical violence or a punishable crime.[153]

The issue of safe spaces is not entirely partisan; while prominent figures on both the progressive "Left" and on moderate to conservative "Right" have spoken out against the problem, the ramifications are most often felt by those on the cultural Right. In 2017, former Obama advisor and civil rights activist Van Jones spoke at the University of Chicago about the state of the country under President Donald Trump and the culture on college campuses.

Jones, representing the views of the students protesting the former President and those who support him, claims that having people associated with him normalized the Administration. In response, Jones both recognizes the merit in having a space free from harassment, physical intimidation, and violence, while also clearly expressing the problem of "ideological safety":

> There is another view, that is now I think more ascendant, which I think is a horrible view. Which is that: I need to be safe ideologically. I need to be safe emotionally. I just need to feel good, all the time, and if someone says something I don't like, then it's a problem for everybody else, including the administration. And I think that is a terrible idea. I don't want you to be safe ideologically. I don't want you to be safe emotionally. I want you to be strong. That's different. I'm not going to pave the jungle for you; put on some boots.[154]

Ideological conformity can result in great success, or it can become incredibly dangerous. If certain ideas, lines of reasoning, and even some people are above criticism, it becomes impossible to address any faults and contradictions in logic. It forces those who acknowledge these faults out of the group in order to maintain its integrity, or worse, pressures them into accepting falsehoods as reality in order to remain within the safe space. This drives a divide between those inside and outside these spaces, creating an ideological in-group vs. out-group mindset.

In addition, labeling these areas as "safe spaces" tacitly implies that spaces outside are "unsafe," fostering an emotional dependence on these areas similar to how cults function. This emotional dependence drives the creation and conversion of new safe spaces, which leads to more emotional dependence in a self-perpetuating cycle of conversion, purge, and creation of a new safe space.

Spaces that claim to be "safe" for, or "caring" toward, marginalized identities ultimately segregate these groups from the wider community or society overall, while reaffirming and focusing on the differences between identity groups, as opposed to focusing on what unites them. The end result is segregation and division—built on the idea of creating inclusive and equitable results, in opposition to the idea of individualism and merit.

Often this takes the form of literal racial segregation. In 2021, a public elementary school in Denver hosted a "families of color playground night" where the minority families could have a space that was safe.[155]

Safe from Whiteness is the implication—teaching those of the target identities to fear and distrust the others, in this case White people. This is not a one-off occasion either: schools, universities, and workplaces across the nation hold "racial affinity" seminars that are segregated by race, among other "identity" characteristics.

Walmart, one of the nation's largest retailers and employers, launched a DEI initiative where, over a multi-day course, employees were taught that one of the most effective ways to facilitate DEI & anti-racism training is to separate the participants into affinity groups, organized by race in order to promote healing from internalized racial oppression.[156]

As this new culture is spread and inherited generationally, this renewed segregation will be paid for with the loss of our civil liberties and the literal blood, pain, and suffering of the young and the easily influenced.

>«

Safe spaces exist to serve an ideology, not the individuals who are claimed to be represented. Even individuals considered target identities can be "acceptably harmed" in order to serve the interests of an identity considered even further oppressed than the initial identity, or even to serve the ideology itself.

The ideological conformity must come above all other needs, most often at the expense of the original intent of the space.

This reality is perhaps best demonstrated through examples. In 2019, the century-old organization the Boy Scouts of America changed its name to Scouts BSA in a bid to become more inclusive and open opportunities for girls. The Boy Scouts, for those unaware, is an organization that has traditionally worked with young boys to mentor them, helping them to develop useful skills, responsibility, respect for their country and community, and a sense of morality as they mature into adulthood.

The change came as a surprise to many, including the rival organization Girl Scouts, which claimed that the decision from the BSA harmed its membership numbers. Other critics argued that young boys are inherently different from young girls in their behavior and development, and removing one of the few spaces in which boys can be socialized away from girls is harmful to their development and the stated goal of the BSA.[157] While the debate over the BSA is largely benign, it does point toward a trend with larger, much graver, consequences.

In June 2021, a man named Scott Smith was arrested at a school board meeting in Loudoun County, Virginia. His crime? Disorderly conduct while protesting a policy from the school board that led to the direct victimization of his daughter. The policy allowed transgender student athletes to use restrooms and changing facilities that "aligned with their gender identity," as opposed to using the facilities for their appropriate sex. The policy aimed to "provide an equitable, safe, and inclusive learning environment for all students. All students shall be treated with dignity and respect, regardless of their sex, sexual orientation, transgender status, or gender identity/expression."[158]

In effect, this policy allows any student to use any bathroom or facility of their choice, so long as they self-identify that they belong in that facility. And, under this policy, a male student entered a girls bathroom wearing a skirt, before sexually assaulting a female student.[159]

In response, the school district superintendent initially claimed that there were no records of assaults in the bathrooms, and that "the predator transgender student or person simply does not exist." The superintendent later resigned over the incident, claiming that his initial response was "misleading."[160]

Let's consider another example where the value of inclusivity came at the expense of an innocent person. Also in June 2021, an incident at a spa led to widespread controversy and civil unrest. At the WI SPA in Los Angeles, a "trans woman" (a man who identifies as a woman) entered a women's changing facility and exposed his male genitalia to the women present, including some children. At the time of the incident, the spa staff denied responsibility, claiming that there was nothing that could be done due to the spa's non-discrimination policy on basis of sexual orientation or identity.[161] An unnamed female complainant in the footage of the incident stated:

> I just want to be clear with you: it's okay for a man to go into the women's section, show his penis around the other women and young little girls, underage, and WI SPA condones that. Is that what you're saying? …
>
> I see a dick. That lets me know he's a man. He is a man, he is not a female. He is not a female.[162]

The incident was widely picked up by political commentators and activists on both sides, eventually building to the point where individuals protesting the spa in support of the women were physically attacked by Los Angeles Antifa agitators, who gathered to "smash transphobia" and "stand up for their 'trans siblings.'" Antifa members, as they are known to do, attacked the opposition protestors and anyone who filmed, shoving or striking some on their heads with blunt objects for merely protesting.[163]

Leftist outlets such as *Slate* were quick to take the side of the violent agitators, claiming that the event was a hoax, until the women from the spa filed a lawsuit against the serial sex offender, forcing *Slate* to issue a correction.[164]

Now, in both of these examples, lone individuals claiming to be transgender in some capacity, took advantage of the law change in order to victimize women and girls in designated female spaces. This is not a condemnation or comment on trans people but shows how predators can easily abuse the new laws. This was surely not the intention of the gender-inclusive laws, but a natural and obvious consequence.

Let's consider a case where the rule changes worked exactly as intended, and how the traditional category of "women" still ends up as the losing party.

In 2014, male Mixed Martial Arts (MMA) fighter Fallon Fox entered the ring against a *female* rival, Tamikka Brents, during the Capital City Cage Wars. Fox is the first MMA fighter to openly identify as transgender (male to female), undergoing surgery and hormone treatment at age thirty. Prior to this, Fox was a United States Navy member, having served as an operations specialist for the *USS Enterprise*. During the two-minute bout, Fox beat "her" opponent badly enough to require seven staples to Brents's head, even fracturing the orbital bone in Brents's skull.

Following the bloody bout, Brents remarked on the overwhelming disparity in power she felt during the match:

> I've fought a lot of women and have never felt the strength that I felt in a fight as I did that night. I can't answer whether it's because she was born a man

> or not because I'm not a doctor. I can only say, I've never felt so overpowered ever in my life and I am an abnormally strong female in my own right. Her grip was different, I could usually move around in the clinch against other females but couldn't move at all in Fox's clinch.[165]

While many, including comedian and podcaster Joe Rogan, commented on the sheer unfairness of allowing fully developed men to participate in combat sports against women due to inherent physiological advantages, supporters of Fox, and Fox "herself" accused critics of the match of being "transphobic" while lauding Fox as "brave." Rogan went on to remark on the stark differences between men and women, down to their chromosomes and genetics that affect all levels of physical development.[166]

If we as a society are going to abandon reality for ideology, who will bear the burden of that change? It seems to be mostly borne by women displaced by transitioned men, and later on by unknowing children who don't know any better.

This is not a one-off occasion. In 2021, twenty-two-year-old transgender swimmer (male to female) Lia Thomas shattered records in the women's swimming category throughout "her" season at University of Pennsylvania. In one day's events, Thomas would break the 100-meter, 200-meter, and 500-meter free time, with results that would qualify Thomas for the National Collegiate Athletic Association (NCAA) women's championships. In the case of the 500-meter free time, Thomas would secure victory an entire 12.9 seconds ahead of the second-place teammate, Anna Sofia Kalandadze.[167]

In the 200-meter free, Thomas would again finish with a nearly seven-second lead over the female competition, setting a new country-wide record for the event.[168] Once again, though the event came under scrutiny and criticism in defense of the competing women, the NCAA stood firm on its commitment to "fair and inclusive competition"—effectively condemning female athletes to second place behind *male* competitors in the *women's* division.

Where's all this heading? It seems to be the erasure of women's categories and spaces. Spaces that were created to protect women and let them thrive without inference from men. In today's culture, by sharp contrast the following achievements in Women's athletics are now held by males:

- One of the best swimmers in the NCAA women's category of 2022[169]
- The top two cyclists of a women's race in 2022.[170]
- In a Washington State cross-country championship event for girls, a male student went from seventy-second place in the boys' division to first place in the girls' division.[171]
- Fans of the popular game show *Jeopardy!* might know that the top recorded "female" contestant is, in fact, male.[172]
- The disgraced and potentially treasonous Biden Administration named a man one of its "Women of the Year" in 2022.[173] In 2023, it honored a man with the International Women of Courage Award.[174]

If that isn't enough, in 2022 a rather portly male won a local New Hampshire Miss America beauty pageant.[175]

Move aside women, and make room for the new and improved "womxn."

》《

How was all of this allowed to occur? How did American, and Western society at large, get to the point where we cannot tell a man from a woman, or we are unwilling admit the differences?

It happened through mass manipulation. Manipulation of language and manipulation of law.

The abuse does not end with adult women, however. Young children introduced to these ideologies just as often end up harmed, sometimes bearing irreparable damage for the rest of their lives.

One consequence of "queering" schools across the nation has been a dramatic increase in the number of youths identifying as transgender. Since 2017, the percentage of thirteen-to-seventeen-year-olds who identify as transgender had more than doubled by 2020, which is more than double the rate of adults reporting the same condition.[176] Along with it, the rate of depressed and suicidal tendencies among transgender youth remains drastically and alarmingly high, with estimates as high as one in three transgender-identifying minors reporting suicide attempts in 2019.[177]

Things get even worse for the children who are pushed down the path of "medical transitioning" in a process proponents call "affirming gender."

There are three general ways in which a person undergoes a gender transition. The first is "social," involving the changing of attire, name, and pronouns. Young boys may wear feminine attire and makeup, while young girls may use masculine names, get short haircuts, and wear chest binders to hide their breasts.

The second method involves a category of drugs called puberty blockers that are often prescribed to gender-confused youths. These drugs are often touted to be able to delay the onset of puberty, "like a pause button," until the child can determine which gender he or she wants to be. And should the transitioning child—sometimes as young as three years old—no longer wish to transition at a later date, then puberty can be resumed as normal and the effects reversed.[178] Or so it's claimed.

These drugs, a notable example being Lupron, are issued as a method of "gender affirming care." There are two major issues that are often left out of the conversation on these treatments.

The first issue being the side effects of these drugs. According to the St. Louis Children's Hospital, which supports so called gender-affirming care:

> By blocking the sex hormones testosterone and estrogen, puberty blockers delay changes that can affect gender expression, including:

- Breast growth
- Facial hair growth
- Periods
- Voice deepening
- Widening hips[179]

This makes sense, as puberty is generally the time period where such secondary sexual characteristics develop. The hospital then goes on to describe some of the potential long-term side effects that should have been listed with the intended effects:

Possible long-term side effects of puberty blockers:

- Lower bone density. To protect against this, we work to make sure every patient gets enough exercise, calcium and vitamin D, which can help keep bones healthy and strong. We also closely monitor patients' bone density.
- Delayed growth plate closure, leading to slightly taller adult height.
- Less development of genital tissue, which may limit options for gender affirming surgery (bottom surgery) later in life.
- Other possible long-term side effects that are not yet known.

Possible short-term side effects of puberty blockers:

- Headache, fatigue, insomnia and muscle aches.
- Changes in weight, mood or breast tissue.
- Spotting or irregular periods (in menstruating patients whose periods are not completely suppressed by puberty blockers).
- For children who want to delay or prevent unwanted physical changes, the mental health benefits of puberty blockers may outweigh these risks.[180]

Lower bone density can lead to a drastic increase in mobility and general developmental complications, with some women who undergo these treatments before and during puberty developing osteoporosis far earlier than expected in the general population. And while some facilities, such as the Seattle Children's Hospital, claim that the puberty blockers "should not" affect fertility,[181] there is no basis for that claim, as both hospitals acknowledge that the medications can stunt the development of genital tissue and organs.

It should be obvious to anyone that "pausing" puberty would affect the development of sexual organs in males and females.

The second issue: these drugs are entirely experimental. Both the Seattle and the St. Louis hospital admit that there are unknown long-term side effects of these treatments. The Seattle hospital further adds that while drugs like Lupron have been approved by the FDA for other uses, they are not approved for treating transgender children.[182]

Why in the name of God, Allah, Zeus, or Cthulhu are we condoning giving untested, development-stunting drugs to children? Moloch might be pleased with you, I suppose. And for added context: the approved use of Lupron is the chemical castration of pedophiles.[183]

Lupron isn't the only method that results in the castration of gender-confused youths. The third method of "gender-affirming care" is through surgery, commonly referred to as "top" or "bottom" surgery.

According to John Hopkins Medicine, top surgery involves either the feminization or masculinization of the chest, which may include the augmentation or removal of breast tissue:

For chest feminization:

- Breast augmentation with implants.
- Breast augmentation with fat grafting.
- Breast augmentation with implants *and* fat grafting.

For chest masculinization:

- Remove breast tissue and overlying skin.
- Eliminate the crease along the bottom of the breast (the inframammary crease).

- Contour the chest and emphasize the pectoral muscles.
- Make the nipples and areolas smaller and reposition them (nipple grafts).
- Remove the nipples entirely depending on patient preferences.[184]

These are not things that can be reversed. And while adults can consent to all manner of cosmetic surgeries from a tattoo to a forked tongue, these are not suitable for identity-confused minors. As no procedure is without risk, these surgeries are certainly no exception. According to Johns Hopkins:

Risks, Complications and Side Effects of Top Surgery

Top surgery scars: For chest masculinization procedures, scars may appear as horizontal lines across the chest, or circles around the areolas. For chest feminization procedures, the scars will be located underneath the breasts. It can take up to 18 months for scars to resolve, and some people elect to have further surgery to minimize them. It is important to avoid sun exposure, which can darken scars and make them more obvious.

Hematoma: Blood can gather in the tissues after surgery and form a clot, with symptoms such as pain, swelling and discoloration as well as an increased risk for infection. Hematomas form in about 1% to 2% of top surgeries.

Seroma: Fluid can collect under the skin. Small seromas may not need any treatment and go away on their own. Seromas in top surgery can be prevented by drains in the surgical area and wearing your compression vest consistently after your procedure.

Infection: This is a rare complication of top surgery, but can happen. Cellulitis in the surgical area may require treatment with oral antibiotics and drainage.

Breakdown of nipple graft:While some skin sloughing is no cause for concern, deeper tissue death (necrosis) can indicate that the graft is not successful and more surgery may be necessary.

Reduced nipple sensitivity:Numbness or tingling can happen if a nerve is disrupted or damaged during surgery. The double incision approach for chest masculinization involves removing and repositioning the nipple, which calls for cutting the nerves. Nipple numbness may improve over time, but full restoration of sensation is unlikely.

Irregular contours: Additional surgery to address chest contour may be called for in up to 32% of top procedures.[185]

Eighteen months for scar tissue to heal, and one in three recipients will need further surgeries to correct contour, assuming nothing else goes wrong. Are you feeling lucky?

And that's only the upper body.

Should one choose to undergo or be subjected to bottom surgery, a whole other set of complications may arise, assuming that regret is not among them.

»«

You can take your gender-confused child to Boston Children's Hospital if your child, his or her doctor, or your child's teacher thinks that your child would be a good candidate for lower-body gender-affirming "care."

If your daughter wants to become your son, the facility will perform what is called a phalloplasty, using skin obtained from elsewhere on the body, typically the arm:

> Phalloplasty is the surgical creation of a penis. In this procedure, surgeons harvest one or more "flaps" of skin and other tissues from a donor site on your body (usually your forearm) and use it to form a penis and urethra.

> The clinicians in the Center for Gender Surgery at Boston Children's Hospital offer phalloplasty as a gender affirmation procedure to eligible patients age 18 and over who have been living in their identified gender full time for at least 12 months. Our skilled team includes specialists in plastic surgery, urology, gender management, and social work who work together to provide a full suite of options for transgender teens and young adults.[186]

While medical centers like the Boston Children's Hospital claim that recipients of these treatments are at least eighteen years of age, Boston Children's Hospital and Children's Hospital Colorado both have these experimental treatments under their "children's" section, and the original iteration of their transgender care page specified "at least 17 years of age."[187]

Should everything go according to plan, the woman turned "man" (because "male" is a sex category, not a gender) will have a non-functioning, non-erect penile-looking appendage. The arm used for the donor skin will look like it had a piece carved out of it, because it did.

Assuming that none of the following happens, as documented by the University of California, San Francisco's Transgender Care guidelines:

> Immediate/early (within one month) complications after free or pedicled flap phalloplasty:

- Wound infections
- Wound breakdown (common)
- Urinary catheter difficulties
- Flap loss (rare)
- Pelvic or groin hematomas
- Rectal injury (rare & serious)

Long-term complications after free or pedicled flap phalloplasty:

- Urethral strictures
- Wound contraction and scarring
- Scars
- Granulation tissue (common)
- Corona flattening (occasionally)[188]

There is also no guarantee that nerves will regain their function after the surgery. Meaning, the grafted pseudo-organ may have no feeling to it at all. And you may still encounter one of the other numerous complications.

In addition, gender-affirming care sometimes involves a hysterectomy, which have been performed on girls as young as seventeen.[189]

Boston Children's Hospital also offers vaginoplasties for young men who want to become women:

What is vaginoplasty?

Vaginoplasty is a procedure in which surgeons create a vagina from your existing genital tissue. Vaginoplasty requires a lifetime commitment to aftercare, because women who have a vaginoplasty will have to dilate their vagina regularly to keep it open.

The clinicians in the Center for Gender Surgery at Boston Children's Hospital offer vaginoplasty as a gender affirmation procedure to eligible patients who have been living in their identified gender full time for at least 12 months.[190]

Assuming nothing goes awry, the new "woman" should have an orifice four inches to six inches deep and a functional urethra opening for urine, again without the guarantee of nerve function—a "neo-vagina," as it's sometimes referred to.

Once again, assuming absolutely nothing goes awry.

In reality, many things can go wrong, and often do.

The main concern of the new woman will be maintaining the new orifice, which will require a lifetime of maintenance and dilation to remain open as the body tries to close it.

Combine that with the chance that after puberty blockers, there may not be enough development of the body to even begin a transitional surgery without the certainty of complications. And the individual might have complications from the top surgery as well!

Are you still feeling lucky?

On April 19, 2023, it was discovered that Dell Children's Medical Center in Austin prescribed puberty blockers to minors as young as eight, gender-affirming surgeries at age ten, and "cross-sex hormones" to minors fourteen and up:

> I follow the WPATH guidelines, the World Professional Association of Transgender Health guidelines, and really what they would say is, the way to go at this age—age 10—would be something like a puberty blocker…and that really stops puberty pretty quickly so that no further development of the secondary sexual characteristics happen. So, things like, there's no real chest development. There's no menstruation. Things like that.

> When you then get to age 14 is when I'll consider some, you know, cross-gender hormones. Fourteen is a reasonable age. Most kids are mature enough to make a relatively informed decision.[191]

This is a barbaric, experimental sex-change procedure leaving adults and some minors as permanent medical patients. Even if some adults choose to consent to this, this is supposedly a treatment for gender dysphoria, not a lifestyle that should be encouraged to young, confused people as a trendy fad.

As graphic as this is, and as much as I considered not including it, it's best that people understand the dark reality of what is being offered to them and their children.

»«

As if the end goal and possible complications along the way were not bad enough, the methods of praxis and indoctrination in these class-rooms often takes the form of abuse.

In some instances, your children might find themselves on a field trip to an Antifa "direct action," protests that often involve the use of mob violence and low-level terrorism against conservatives or non-progressive political actors.

In August 2021, a Project Veritas undercover journalist uncovered a Sacramento public high school teacher, Gabriel Gipe, who admitted to grooming his students into radical far-left extremist revolutionaries in his lessons—unbeknownst to the school district or the parents:

> Yeah. I have 180 days to turn them [students] into revolutionaries....
>
> So, you know, it's like my wife and I have been polit-ical organizers, I've been organizing since I was thir-teen. And I've been in a ton of different [Antifa] orga-nizations, and I've been on the front lines and gone back and forth and my wife is the same way....
>
> So like, when there's right-wing rallies and stuff then, we like, we'll create an opposition to that. Yeah. So, and Sacramento, as a city itself, is incredibly diverse,

but we're surrounded by a bunch of right-wing rednecks.[192]

The child soldier program is not just reserved for middle and high schoolers large enough to carry signs and strong enough to throw bricks or cans of soup.

In July 2022, a public elementary school in Denver organized an event for kindergarteners and first-graders (approximately four to seven years of age). The event itself was part of the Black Lives Matter School Week of Action, which was endorsed by schools and educational programs across the nation. The purpose of the event? To teach young children about the core values of the BLM movement, primary among them being "restorative justice, transgender affirming, queer affirming, globalism, and the disruption of western nuclear family dynamics."[193]

A bunch of woke bullshit.

If you're fortunate enough to avoid having your child turned into a violent accomplice for race-based activism, congratulations.

May you also be fortunate enough to avoid your son or daughter being given lessons on the "inclusiveness" of sex toys in their sex-ed class, or a field trip to the local drag stripper for story-time.

Think that's hyperbole? Maybe a bit of an over-exaggeration?

On December 7, 2022, undercover journalist organization Project Veritas released a video of Joseph Bruno, the dean of students at Francis W. Parker School in Chicago. In the exposé, Bruno reveals that one of the coolest parts of his job is educating the students on the use of sex toys, and the merits of lube vs. spit.

> So, I've been the Dean for four years. During Pride—we do a Pride Week every year—I had our LGBTQ+ Health Center come in [to the classroom]. They were passing around butt-plugs and dildos to my students—talking about queer sex, using lube versus using spit.
>
> They're just, like, passing around dildos and butt-plugs. The kids are just playing with 'em, looking at

> 'em.… They're like, "How does this butt-plug work? How do we do—like, how does this work?' That's a really cool part of my job.

> We had a Drag Queen come in—pass out cookies and brownies and do photos.[194]

In no way, shape, or form is this acceptable for minors. This is not even reproductive education, which is what most people understand "sex-ed" classes to be. This is overt grooming, masked as sex-ed and LGBTQIA+ studies. A rainbow-colored Trojan horse gifted to children, with sexual predators lying in wait.

Parents across the entire country have begun to realize and oppose the grooming of their children by radical LGBTQIA+ activists. Just a few months earlier, in Dallas, a gay bar called Mr. Misster came under scrutiny after hosting an event called "Drag the Kids to Pride," a drag queen show advertised as "family friendly."

Despite the family friendly claim, sexually provocative performers danced under signs reading "It's not gonna lick itself!" while children watched from a few feet away, while other children were escorted down the runway alongside the adult entertainers.[195]

If adults want to cross-dress at bars and perform for other adults, that is one thing. Nobody cares. But at no point should children be exposed to these kinds of sexualized displays. And yet, progressive LGBTQIA+ activists insist on involving young children in these situations. Following the backlash to the event, the organizers claimed to be the recipient of "homophobic and transphobic remarks and vile accusations at these children and parents." The police were called, but only to help "disperse the protesting crowd in a safe manner" according to the Dallas Police Department.[196]

This is the bait-and-switch tactic often used to defend the indefensible. Groups and malicious actors targeting children with sexual content, using allegations of "homophobia" or "transphobia" to diffuse any and all criticism.

It is no accident or coincidence. While certainly not all—or even the majority—of gay or transgender people support these abuses, there are well-funded, well-organized institutions seeking to subvert the values of the next generation, create race and gender accomplices out of them, and groom them into participating in sexualized situations.

> We're dressing up, we're shaking our hips, and we're finding our light—even in the fluorescents. We're reading books while we read each other's looks, and we're leaving a trail of glitter that won't ever come out of the carpet.-'Lil Miss Hot Mess, PhD candidate at NYU, and a Drag Queen Story hour activist[197]

The most terrifying part: as society becomes more dominated by DEI and LGBTQIA+ ideology, there will be increased pressures on law to enforce these ideals, even at the expense of our liberties. On April 15, 2023, Washington State passed SB 5599, a bill to legally enforce and safeguard the gender transition of minors under the guise of "protected healthcare." If parents deny this treatment to their child, they may be held criminally responsible for "abusing" their child by not chemically or surgically castrating their child.

And the final nail in the hopefully metaphorical coffin: should a child seeking to transition run away from home, the state has no obligation to inform the parents of the child's whereabouts.[198] Washington State can kidnap your child and sterilize him or her without notifying you, until you receive a court summons for neglect and abuse because you told your child, "Wait until you're eighteen."

So, what has been the cost of all this supposed diversity, equity, and inclusion? A few scores of battered and displaced women by transwomen, and women's sport becoming dominated by men. Meanwhile, in kindergarten through high school children are being indoctrinated into a worldview where they are encouraged to sterilize and scar themselves if they are not a stereotype of a masculine man or feminine woman. At the same time, they're instructed on how to destroy the nuclear family and violently demonstrate for radical-left causes, while they're unable to define "woman." And nearly half contemplate suicide before and after their gender treatment. Meanwhile, those warning of these consequences have their civil rights unconstitutionally infringed upon as the state becomes an accomplice to radical activists.

In any war, truth is the first casualty. After truth, it is those most victimized by the aggressing faction, in this case women and children, the categories that used to be the most protected in Western value systems. The last victim in this war will be the death and demise of American values, and the country along with it.

6

THE AMERICAN EXPERIMENT—
NEGATIVE RIGHTS ARE
POSITIVE FOR HUMANS

To understand how critical race theory (CRT), diversity, equity, and inclusion (DEI), and the other woke ideologies came into existence, it's important to first understand America as a concept. Examine the very beginning of our country, with the preamble to the Declaration of Independence, written by Thomas Jefferson and vetted by those two stalwarts of the American Revolution, Ben Franklin and John Adams. The document begins:

> We hold these truths to be self-evident, that *all men are created equal* [emphasis added], that they are endowed by their creator with certain unalienable rights, that among these are Life, Liberty, and the pursuit of Happiness. That to secure these rights, Governments are instituted among Men, deriving their just powers from the consent of the governed, —That whenever any Form of Government becomes destructive of these ends, it is the Right of the People to alter

or abolish it, and to institute new Government, laying its foundation on such principles and organizing its powers in such form, as to them shall seem most likely to effect their Safety and Happiness.[199]

When one considers the entirety of human history, the ideas expressed in this single paragraph may be among the most consequential words ever written. The idea that all men (and now, of course, women) are created equal was the greatest blow ever struck against any hierarchy created by humans. Enshrined in our founding document was the belief that every person is born with certain rights, namely those of life, liberty, and the ability to pursue individual happiness. The purpose of government itself was the protection of those God-given rights. And finally, if the government failed to protect these rights, it could and *should* be altered or abolished. This belief overturned thousands of years of doctrine, used by lands both large and small, claiming that the rulers derived their power from some supreme deity.

The concept of "individual liberty," thus became one of the founding principles of our country. And each person is free to determine how to best express that liberty, as long as the expression of such liberty does not unduly impinge on the rights of another person. In other words, the origin of our natural rights come from a God who is higher than any government power. That's why our Founders, while they did not endorse any single religion, believed that some form of religious belief was essential to the stability of the new country.

And yet it is without doubt that from the start of the Revolutionary War in 1776 until the Civil War and Lincoln's Emancipation Proclamation of January 1, 1863, that we had deeply failed to live up to this ideal. If one genuinely believed that all men are equal, there could be no rational argument to justify the enslavement of the African people. Lincoln understood that the institution of slavery was in direct conflict with the ideals of the young nation and was a lifelong opponent of the barbaric institution. (It must also be noted that

Lincoln did not believe that Congress had the power to abolish slavery, except perhaps outside of the federal enclave of Washington, D.C.)

Even before his ascent to the presidency, Lincoln was best known as one of the country's most passionate opponents of slavery. Lincoln felt that the existence of slavery relegated the ideals of America to empty, hypocritical platitudes. He also felt that if the idea of slavery was not rejected, then the rights of all men would be restricted to an ever increasingly small group of people. From a letter that Lincoln sent to his good friend, Joshua Speed, on August 24, 1855:

> Our progress in degeneracy appears to me to be pretty rapid. As a nation, we begin by declaring that "all men are created equal." We now practically read it "all men are created equal, except negroes." When the Know-Nothings get control, it will read "all men are created equal, except negroes, foreigners, and Catholics." When it comes to this I should prefer emigrating to some country where they make no pretense of loving liberty—to Russia, for instance, where despotism can be taken pure, and without the base alloy of hypocrisy.[200]

Following the abolition of slavery and the end of the Civil War, civil rights were vigorously enforced during the two terms of President Ulysses S. Grant, but the contested election of 1876 resulted in the "Great Betrayal" of the newly freed slaves and federal troops were removed from the South. This allowed Southern politicians—almost exclusively Democrats—to enact the legal segregation of Jim Crow laws, as well as create the domestic terror force of the Ku Klux Klan.

In 1896, the constitutionality of the Jim Crow "separate, but equal" laws were presented to the United States Supreme Court in the infamous case of *Plessy v. Ferguson*.[201] Homer Plessy, a man who was one-eighth Black (12.5 percent) took a seat in a White railcar, even though Plessy was considered Black. After being arrested and forced to relocate to the "Colored Person" seating, he challenged the arrest based on the claim that it violated his civil rights. (In the Democrat-controlled South of the 1890s, being 87.5 percent White meant you were Black in the eyes of the law.)

The law was ruled constitutional by a seven-to-one decision (one justice did not vote). The Court found that the segregation of people did not violate equal protection, as long as both races were provided facilities that were "separate, but equal." However, in practice, the facilities open to Whites were not equal to those provided to Blacks.

The dissent by Justice John Marshall Harlan, though, is what many generations of civil rights activists would base their fight for freedom on in the decades to come. Justice Harlan wrote:

> The white race deems itself to be the dominant race in this country. And so it is, in prestige, in achievements, in education, in wealth, and in power. So, I doubt not, it will continue to be for all time, if it remains true to its great heritage, and holds fast to the principles of constitutional liberty. But in view of the constitution, in the eye of the law, there is in this country no superior, dominant, ruling class of citizens. There is no caste here. Our constitution is color-blind, and neither knows nor tolerates classes among citizens. In respect of civil rights, all citizens are equal before the law. The humblest is the peer of the most powerful. The law regards man as man, and takes no account of his surroundings or of his color when his civil rights as guaranteed by the supreme law of the land are involved. It is therefore to be regretted that this high tribunal, the final expositor of the fundamental law of the land, has reached the conclusion that it is competent for a state to regulate the enjoyment by citizens of their civil rights solely upon the basis of race.[202]

It's important to highlight these racial injustices of the past, as well as the relatively small number of Whites who believed in genuine equality. Yet, our culture of free speech was such that even though Justice Harlan's opinion was so far out of the mainstream, no move was made to silence him (such as the Big Tech platforms often do today), and he remained on the bench, issuing his various dissents, until his death in 1911.

Let's discuss some of the other legal injustices that were allowed in the wake of *Plessy v. Ferguson*. A Missouri law from 1929 held that, "Separate free schools shall be established for the education of children of African descent; and it shall be unlawful for any colored children to attend any white school, or any white child to attend a colored school."[203] A 1930 law in Birmingham, Alabama, read, "It shall be unlawful for a negro and white person to play together with each other in any game of cards or dice, dominoes, or checkers."[204]

The mind boggles to read some of these laws from the South in the early twentieth century. How much of a threat were children sitting in classrooms together, or adults sitting down to play a game of cards, dice, dominoes, or checkers? It seems as if the racists of yesteryear, and those of today, have the same fear: that people of different races might sit together for education or recreation, and find that they're more alike than different.

There is no doubt that racism has significantly affected the lives of millions of Americans in the past.

But that fact does not detract from the two steps we need to take now. First, we must acknowledge how far we have come at this juncture, and second, we must figure out the best strategies as we continue to move forward.

»«

Few will contest the criticism that many parts of American history are not properly covered in school textbooks, particularly those dealing with our ugly past of race riots. What may be the worst race riot in American history happened between May 31 and June 1, 1921, in Tulsa, Oklahoma.[205]

At the time, Tulsa was a growing city with a population of over 100,000 people, with roughly 10 percent of the population being Black. Most of the Black residents resided in the Greenwood District, with so many successful Black businesses—such as doctor's offices, restaurants, libraries, and churches—that it was often referred to as the Black Wall Street. The tragedy of what eventually enfolded is especially acute when considering that this success came approximately sixty years after the start of the American Civil War.

On May 31, 1921, a nineteen-year-old Black shoeshine man named Dick Rowland entered an elevator with a seventeen-year-old White girl named Sarah Page, who was working as an elevator operator. It is unclear exactly what happened during the short elevator ride. An accusation was made that Rowland attempted to rape Page, causing her to scream, while others claim that Rowland had simply stepped on her foot. Rowland was arrested by the police and by the evening there were rumors of an impending lynching being planned for the young man.

By nightfall, several hundred White people had gathered outside the jail, demanding that the sheriff hand Rowland over to the lynch mob. The sheriff refused. Shortly afterward, a large group of armed Black men showed up, offering themselves to the sheriff as extra protection for Rowland. The sheriff declined this offer as well. As the potential for violence seemed to escalate with the growing White mob, the armed Black Tulsans repeated their offer of assistance. Again, the sheriff declined the offer.

While the armed Black Tulsans were leaving, someone in the mob attempted to disarm one of the Black men, a shot was fired, and mayhem ensued.

Thousands of armed White Tulsans ransacked Greenwood, killing an estimated fifty to 300 people, most of whom were Black. The Black residents were armed, but they were outnumbered and outgunned. There were reports of Greenwood being besieged by airplanes dropping incendiaries and Whites on the ground using machine guns. Thirty-five city blocks were razed, more than twenty-four grocery stores, thirty-one restaurants, and 1,200 homes were destroyed. More than 10,000 people—practically the entire Black population of Tulsa—were left homeless.

Besides the loss of human life, an additional devastating effect of the Tulsa Race Riot was the loss of generational wealth, the money that parents could have passed on to their children to give the next generation an advantage. Imagine what an example the Black residents of Tulsa could have shown the country, how in sixty years a people could climb from slavery to success.

Many would say—and I would agree—that this was an appalling act of racism, and we should teach our children about it.

If this evolution of the Blacks of Tulsa had been allowed to take place, it might have looked similar to the trajectory of many different ethnic groups in our country, from the Irish, Jews, and Italians of the nineteenth century to many of our newest immigrant groups, such as Vietnamese, Indian, and other Asian groups.

But it's worth mentioning that there's something that needs to be examined even more deeply: the idea of individual identity versus group identity. It is in this difference, in which we most clearly see the clash between the ideals of Dr. Martin Luther King, Jr. and the current generation of activists pushing CRT.

Dr. King saw and preached to people as individuals, each responsible for his own actions. If one believes in the uniqueness—as well as the rights—of the individual, there is simply no room for racism. In the individualist mindset, there is simply no space for race.

When looking back on, and reading, history, it appears to be that the worst atrocities are committed by people who look at others through a group lens rather than an individual one. Thus, the European slavers and African slavers looked at other African tribes and saw only slaves. They did not see individuals of equal worth or value.

Hitler and the Nazis looked at the Jews, gays, and gypsies and saw groups of creatures they believed were subhuman. They did not see individuals. The same can be said of the Chinese Communist Party and the Uyghur Muslims, forced into camps and subjected to violations of human rights so cruel that they are beyond the imagination of those unaware of history.

The advocates of Jim Crow laws saw people only in shades of white and black. They did not see individuals.

Whether or not Dick Rowland did anything criminal in that elevator with Sarah Page, the Whites of Tulsa saw only a trespass against the White race by a member of the Black race, and believed the punishment must be delivered to every Black person in the city. The Whites of Tulsa did not see the Blacks in their city as individuals. The vengeance for which they so hungered must be against the group, not even giving the accused a chance to defend himself in a court of law.

I am terrified of those pushing CRT because I see in them the same tunnel vision that acknowledges only groups, and not individuals. They have the same myopic view of slavers, Nazis, and segregationists, with the fervor of the mobs who would burn anyone deemed a "witch" at the stake with glee.

There's a popular story called "Two Wolves," which is usually attributed to an ancient Cherokee legend.[206] In the story, a grandfather says to his grandson, "There are two wolves within every person, and they are always fighting. One wolf is anger and despair. The other is love and hope. Which one wins?"

The grandson is unable to answer.

"The one you feed," says the grandfather, then warns. "Be careful of which wolf you feed."

The metaphor of the two wolves is an excellent description of the journey that every human being must take in this life. The path of the individual exemplified by the work of Dr. Martin Luther King, Jr. leads to love and hope, while the path of CRT leads to anger and despair.

Let us look at how we might feed the better wolves of our nature.

»«

How do we overcome the natural human tendency to regard with favor those who look and act like us and approach with some suspicion those who do not? This trait has served us well for hundreds of thousands of years when we lived in relatively small groups of people, hoping to quickly identify friend from foe, but in today's modern world we don't require that behavior anymore.

I'm not going to condemn this trait, which has assured the survival of human beings over the millennia, but I do agree that a new behavior is needed to replace it in some social situations.

For me, the answer—as provided by American history—is the idea of a meritocracy.

What is a meritocracy?

It is a system in which those individuals who work harder than others and who demonstrate a higher aptitude or achievement than their peers, deserve greater rewards than those who do not have those skills. Hard work should be rewarded. The most competent should advance. Most people would agree that it is "just" for people to get what they deserve. If I pay a hundred dollars for a concert ticket, my expectation is that I will be listening to an accomplished musician, not a middle-schooler just learning the clarinet. If I buy a ticket for a major league baseball game, I don't expect the starting pitcher will be a sophomore from the local high school team.

However, the idea of a "just" outcome can only exist in a society that permits individual liberty. The choices one makes will inevitably lead different people to different outcomes. In such a system, those with the highest degree of competence, passion, and work ethic will rise to the top, resulting in the greatest possible good for the largest number of people. This is the justification for competition and the basis of the "free market." As described by James Truslow Adams in his 1931 book, *The Epic of America*:

> The American Dream is that dream of a land in which life should be better and richer and fuller for everyone, with opportunity for each according to ability or achievement. It is a difficult dream for the European upper classes to interpret adequately, and too many of us ourselves have grown weary and mistrustful of it. It is not a dream of motor cars and high wages merely, but a dream of social order in which each man and each woman shall be able to attain to the fullest stature of which they are innately capable, and

be recognized by others for what they are, regardless
of the fortuitous circumstances of birth or position.[207]

The benefit of a meritocracy, as described by Truslow, is a system that does not guarantee wealth or success to any group or individual. A meritocracy, by its very definition, can have no favored groups or individuals. Meritocracy concerns itself solely with the potential of the individual, and the best societies are those that erect or permit the least amount of barriers for the individual to succeed. This type of system relies on the work ethic and resourcefulness of the citizenry, requiring a commitment to the hard work that is necessary for success.

It is this ability to build a life for oneself, largely unrestricted by class boundaries, that led to America being dubbed the Land of Opportunity. Whether a native-born citizen or an immigrant escaping war, poverty, or persecution, the notion that anyone could succeed—regardless of his past or birth status—distinguished the United States from other countries that restricted social and economic mobility.

This philosophy, unique in world history, is memorialized in the poem, *The New Colossus*, placed at the base of the Statue of Liberty in New York harbor. It reads:

> Not like the brazen giant of Greek fame,
> With conquering limbs astride from land to land;
> Here at our sea-washed, sunset gates shall stand
> A mighty woman with a torch, whose flame
> Is the imprisoned lightning, and her name
> Mother of exiles. From her beacon-hand
> Glows world-wide welcome; her mild eyes command
> The air bridged harbor that twin cities frame.
> "Keep ancient lands, your storied pomp!" cries she
> With silent lips. "Give me your tired, your poor,
> Your huddled masses yearning to breathe free,
> The wretched refuse of your teeming shore.
> Send these, the homeless, tempest-tost to me,
> I lift my lamp beside the golden door![208]

When one looks at the data on immigration to this country, a remarkably consistent picture emerges. In 1860, there were approximately five million immigrants in the United States, comprising about 13 percent of the population. Until the 1920s, immigrants comprised about 12 percent to 15 percent of the population.[209] After the infamous Immigration Act of 1924 passed—bankrolled by the Carnegie, Mellon, and Rockefeller families, and given intellectual cover by Harvard and Stanford Universities, as well as the Eugenics Office at the Cold Springs Harbor Lab, run by the United States government—these numbers dropped precipitously.[210] By 1970, only about 5 percent of the population were immigrants, an astonishing hundred-year low.[211] However, the latest numbers show a rebound to historic levels, with the latest figures from 2020 revealing that 15 percent of the population are immigrants.[212]

The data clearly shows that America has long been a country welcoming to immigrants from various walks of life, cultures, and backgrounds. No country in history has such a generous immigration system, which gives millions of immigrants the opportunity to pursue their economic and personal dreams in freedom.

Data from the Migration Policy Institute show that immigrants do especially well in the United States. The comparison between US-born adults and all immigrants shows that there is barely any difference (around 35 percent of immigrants and US-born adults) for those obtaining a bachelor's degree or higher. However, when we break down the data to look solely at recently arrived immigrants, we see that approximately 50 percent of this group earned a bachelor's degree or higher.[213] (Recently arrived immigrants to America have an even more positive view of their possibilities for success than native-born Americans or those immigrants who arrived earlier.)[214]

This information makes complete sense when we consider the idea of meritocracy, which is one of the factors that makes the United States so attractive to those from other countries. Immigrants flock to our country because they believe in this idea of meritocracy. They believe that the competition allowed in this country will create the best ideas, products, and outcomes, especially for those willing to put in the work. Financial freedom goes hand in hand with all other types of freedom.

It's important to understand how this freedom allows each individual to live according to his or her unique preferences. Each of us has a vision of our perfect life, driven by such factors as our environment, upbringing, experiences, personal desires, and abilities. This unique combination will determine the opportunities available to us. Even identical twins, born and raised in the same household, will not experience life in the very same manner, nor will they have the same interests and abilities. The twins I have known generally have significantly different personalities, often one being more outgoing than the other, one preferring academics, while the other prefers athletics, despite the fact that they share the exact same genes.

Taken to its logical end, no two individuals—even if they share 100 percent of the same genes—will live the same life, nor would anyone want that outcome. As a result, we would not expect their end result to be the same, either. This disparity is not the result of any active discrimination, but the result of their own experiences, interests, and life choices. It is foolish to expect all people to choose the same life path and to do equally well in the same situations. They will be presented with different opportunities, be interested in different pursuits, and have different aptitudes. It is madness to believe that we might understand how other people should conduct their own lives.

This explanation is not to dismiss the corrosive effect of government or socially enforced segregation or discrimination. In fact, America's strong commitment to the freedom of the individual makes it clear why Americans have generally viewed any limitation of a person's freedom to pursue his own individual course through life as an evil which must be vigorously confronted and defeated. If an individual is not free to participate in the society around him because of active discrimination or segregation, this will deny him the opportunities he may otherwise have had.

However, we must be careful not to claim that all disparity or inequity—particularly when comparing demographics—is the result of active or passive discrimination.

Let's take a look at the difference between men and women in employment. According to the US Department of Labor, 56.4 percent of full-time workers are men, with 45.6 percent being women.[215]

For part-time workers, the numbers are flipped, 37 percent are men and 63 percent are women.[216]

It is not sexist to observe that men seem to value full-time employment more than women, in broad demographic terms. That's neither a good nor a bad thing.

If one compares the health of men to women, women are generally healthier and live several years longer than men.[217] Is that a direct result of their making different choices, valuing social relations and connections to a greater extent than men, who usually have far fewer friends as they move through life?[218] While it may be worthwhile to discuss the employment differences between men and women, it seems that equal attention should be focused on the disparity of years of actual life between men and women. If we fail to address that issue as well, we are not getting a fully rounded discussion of these issues or of the consequences of our choices.

»«

The final pillar to cover in this chapter on American society is the concept of negative rights.

One can define negative rights as the individual's inherent ability to act or obtain something without the outside interference of others. For example, we have the right to life, free speech, private property, and free association, as long as these efforts do not interfere with the ability of others to do the same.

However, most of the discussion of rights in popular discourse has nothing to do with the idea of negative rights, but instead concerns itself with claims of a "right" to healthcare or a "right" to housing. While these may be laudable goals, we need to ask ourselves how much such rights might infringe on a person's "negative rights." Perhaps the greatest popular example of this tension is the exchange between Canadian professor and author Jordan Peterson and English newswoman Cathy Newman on the limits of free speech:

> CATHY NEWMAN: Why should your right to freedom of speech trump a trans-person's right not to be offended?

> JORDAN PETERSON: Because, in order to be able to think, you have to risk being offensive.[219]

If we are to remain citizens in a free society there are certain lines that our government must not cross and that must be respected by the greater society. If these guard rails are not present, we risk becoming simple subjects to the changing whims of our rulers, whether in the government or popular culture.

The concept of rights can be traced back to the philosophers John Locke and Thomas Hobbes, and it is instructive to understand how each of them viewed these rights as existing in the "state of nature," independent of any governmental or societal structure. In his work *Second Treatise of Government*, Locke describes these rights existing as part of the default nature of human beings: "A state of perfect freedom to order their actions and dispose of their possessions and persons, as they think fit, within the bounds of the law of nature; without asking leave or depending on the will of any other man."[220]

Hobbes likens this state of freedom to animals of the same species, who are gifted with nothing more than their natural talents and the gifts of nature around them. Individual creatures will rise above others due to their abilities to gather food and materials for shelter and interact with other creatures. In civilization there's the additional benefit of laws which prevent depredations against the weak, giving all the ability to compete on a level playing field, where the rewards flow to the talented and hardworking. People will acquire resources through their own labor and trade, according to their desires and inclinations, and interact with other people as they see fit.

In a similar vein, an individual has the same inherent right to protect his resources from being stolen or destroyed. An individual also has the right to defend his person from danger, as well as a right to defend members of his family.

The following could be classified as the five essential "negative rights" as the foundation to American society:

> **Right to Life.** Individuals have a right to life, in which they are not under the subjugation, rule, or possession of another. As such, individuals have the autonomy to direct their own lives as they see fit, and society cannot take this right from them without the due process of a tribunal conducted by other free people.
>
> **Right to Use One's Voice.** Individuals have the right to speak their mind, without suppression from a higher authority, and within a society that values the exercise of those rights.
>
> **Right to Obtain, Own, and Trade Property.** Individuals have the right to gather and own resources, as well as engage with others in mutual and consensual trade of these resources. The most just societies also have a culture that encourages and celebrates these exchanges between free people because they understand that this activity results in the greatest mutual benefit to society.
>
> **Right of Association.** Individuals have the right to freely associate or not associate with people, as they choose. In a genuinely free society, the culture embraces and celebrates those individuals with the widest circle of associations, while also respecting the right of those—who for personal reasons which they are allowed to keep private—do not have a large circle of people with whom they associate.
>
> **Right to Self-Defense.** As each person is a sovereign in control of his physical body, thoughts, and possessions, it follows that he also possesses the right of a sovereign

to defend his property. A society based on the essential rights of the individual also celebrates those who heroically defend their interests, while condemning those who trespass upon the rights of another.

Locke believed that because all people in their "natural state" possessed such liberties, there was a state of true equality between them, as all the relations between them would be by necessity reciprocal. In this state of reciprocity, none could be subordinate to another, as each possessed the same liberty.

Even in this "natural state" where people have their rights, they do not have license to impede the rights of others. When one does infringe on the rights of another, there must be a system to redress grievances of the victim and penalize the aggressor. Locke considered this system, meant to maintain the public good and peace of the commonwealth, to be the origin of all political power.

It is essentially from these negative rights that what we refer to as our "civil rights" have come into existence. The difference is that civil rights are backed by the political power of the state to preserve the rights of the individual within society. Both Hobbes and Locke agreed that civilization was not the natural state of mankind but varied in some key areas. Hobbes argued that individuals do not have a duty to any other creature. By contrast, Locke argued that individuals have a "natural duty" to respect the rights of others, in order for society to keep from devolving into a state of internal warfare and strife.[221] As a personal preference, I support Locke's view of this natural duty to respect others, and yet I also believe that an individual must be free to live as Hobbes envisioned, without any duty to others.

In America, these civil rights are forever enshrined in the Constitution's first ten amendments, the Bill of Rights. These amendments are remarkably brief, but clearly delineate the rights of the individual in respect to the state, as well as assert that these rights don't come from the state but are the natural inheritance of humanity. They are:

Amendment I. Congress shall make no law respecting an establishment of religion, or prohibiting the free exercise thereof; or abridging the freedom of speech, or the press; or the right of the people peacefully to assemble, and to petition the Government for a redress of grievances.

Amendment II. A well regulated militia, being necessary to the security of a free State, the right of the people to keep and bear Arms, shall not be infringed.

Amendment III. No soldier shall, in time of peace be quartered in any house, without the consent of the owner, nor in time of war, but in a manner prescribed by law.

Amendment IV. The right of the people to be secure in their persons, houses, papers, and effects, against unreasonable searches and seizures, shall not be violated, and no warrants shall issue, but upon probable cause, supported by oath or affirmation, and particularly describing the place to be searched, and the persons or things to be seized.

Amendment V. No person shall be held to answer for a capital, or otherwise infamous crime, unless on a presentment or indictment of a grand jury, except in cases arising in the land or naval forces, or in the militia, when in actual service in time of war or public danger; nor shall any person be subjected for the same offense to be twice put in jeopardy of life or limb; nor shall be compelled in any criminal case to be a witness against himself, nor be deprived of life, liberty, or property, without due process of law; nor shall private property be taken for public use, without just compensation.

Amendment VI. In all criminal prosecutions, the accused shall enjoy the right to a speedy and public trial, by an impartial jury of the state and district wherein the crime shall have been committed, which district shall have been previously ascertained by law, and to be informed of the nature and cause of the accusation; to be confronted with the witnesses against him; to have compulsory process for obtaining witnesses in his favor, and to have the assistance of counsel for his defense.

Amendment VII. In suits at common law, where the value in controversy shall exceed twenty dollars, the right of trial by jury shall be preserved, and no fact tried by a jury, shall be otherwise reexamined in any court of the United States, than according to the rules of the common law.

Amendment VIII. Excessive bail shall not be required, nor excessive fines imposed, nor cruel and unusual punishments inflicted.

Amendment IX. The enumeration of the Constitution, of certain rights, shall not be construed to deny or disparage others retained by the people.

Amendment X. The powers not delegated to the United States by the Constitution, nor prohibited by it to the states, are reserved to the states respectively, or to the people.[222]

One might ask, What distinguishes negative rights from positive rights? The simplest way to understand this difference is that with a negative right, you are *free to do* something—period. With a positive right, you *have been given permission* to do something by some superior entity, which has the power to take that right away from you.

Let's consider the claim that "healthcare is a human right." If someone falls and injures his leg and it's bleeding profusely, where does he get healthcare?

Under a natural rights theory, he could certainly voice his concerns about the injury, seek materials to dress the wound, and bargain with others for a mutual exchange of services. But by the time all this took place, he might be dead.

This is clearly an example of where the natural rights theory offers little practical assistance.

Healthcare requires human labor to create, transport, and administer the medical supplies. Since the emergency will render the calm deliberation necessary for bargaining an impossibility, our society has made an exception in these circumstances by providing help in situations requiring immediate medical attention. And yet, what do we decide to do when the question moves beyond those who require immediate medical assistance?

Any time a positive right is asserted, that assertion requires the production of a product, or the performance of a service. Materials and labor are not infinite, nor are they necessarily proportional to demand. If there are a hundred doses of a drug, and there are 1,000 individuals with a right to them, what do we do? We must somehow come up with 900 more doses.

This same logic applies to any other entitlement awarded to an individual. It requires the payment of a third party to create, maintain, or distribute the entitlement.

If the third party is the government, the labor and investment must still come first from individuals. The government will then enforce this taking under the threat of harm by the state, to later redistribute as it sees fit.

A clear understanding of philosophical perspectives is necessary to fully understand the risk that CRT poses to our world. I have sketched in simple, easy to understand language, that under our Constitution, our rights do not come from the government. Instead, governments are established to protect our rights, though they often fail to do so.

One of the deceptive tactics employed by the proponents of CRT, is to cloak their true intentions behind deceptive words like "justice" or "equity," which will mean different things to different people.

As George Orwell once wrote, "The great enemy of clear language is insincerity. When there is a gap between one's real and one's declared aims, one turns as it were instinctively to long words and exhausted idioms, like a cuttlefish squirting out ink."[223]

Keep this in mind as you read this book, or any other book, regardless of the point of view. In this case, when researching CRT, the concept of clear language should be in play. If you read passages that are unclear, or vague, it is possible you are being deceived. The professed intentions of the writing may well hide the true intentions of the authors. Vladimir Lenin, the first communist leader of the Soviet Union once wrote, "Give us the child for eight years and it will be a Bolshevik forever."[224]

Is it any wonder why "queering schoolhouses" with the addition of divisive "anti-racist" propaganda to grade-schoolers has become such a hotly debated issue? And that the proponents of CRT wanted to infiltrate a massive toy company and get to children before they even started kindergarten?

Really makes you wonder what's going on. We are trapped in a war of culture—a cultural revolution. And the stakes are American culture itself and the children who grow up in the country as the next generation.

7

THE MARXIST ROOTS OF CRITICAL THEORY AND WOKENESS

It is important to understand that critical race theory (CRT) is an ideology and worldview based in Marxism, which divides the world into "oppressed" and "oppressor" classes. Those who possess or uphold "Whiteness" are the oppressor group; those who lack "Whiteness," or do not uphold its values are the oppressed group.

Marxism is a philosophical doctrine developed by Karl Marx, which focused on class struggle within a society as the main focal point. In its classic application, societies could be broken down into their two main classes: those who own the means of production (bourgeoise) and the workers who run the machines (proletariat). In Marx's view, these two classes were permanently at odds with each other, and revolution is the only way to break this vicious cycle of exploitation.

As with any philosophy, there were different schools of thought. Trotsky and Stalin fought out what communism meant in the Soviet Union, and Mao put his own stamp on Chinese communism in the 1950s, eventually changed by Deng Xiaoping in the 1970s.

However, all of them shared the central theme of class struggle solved through a revolution in which the proletariat overthrows the bourgeoise.

CRT is an offshoot of the Frankfurt School of Critical Theory, which developed a Marxist Studies program back in 1933 Germany, before being shut down by the Nazi Party.[225] The National Socialists and the Communists never had much love for each other. Both groups sought to obtain ultimate power and both condoned violence, and thus one could not allow the other to exist.

However, following its forced closure by the Nazi Party, the Marxist Frankfurt School of Critical Theory was re-formed at the world's second-most-welcoming place for communism after the Soviet Union—Columbia University in New York City. But the class-struggle framework didn't work as well in the United States as it did in Europe, given the ability of so many to move from the poor to middle or upper class within a few decades.

Something had to replace the concept of class struggle in America, and that ended up being the racial struggle, which has a sad, unfortunate, and very real history in the United States—ripe for exploitation by racial Marxist agitators.

CRT was birthed from the concept of critical legal studies (CLS), which began as an effort by a small group of leftist academics to identify the ways in which racism had become embedded into American legal structures, and how to change those structures into a more equitable system.

As a growing set of scholarly essays emerged under the twin banners of CLS and CRT, two common principles guided and linked the works:

1. Accepting and understanding how a White Supremacist regime had been created to subordinate "people of color" in America, and
2. Demonstrat[ing] the desire to understand, and ultimately change the bond between racial power and law in America. *Critical Race Theory: The Key Writings That formed the Movement*[226]

From the perspective of a critical race theorist, the doctrine of color-blindness is as morally despicable as the white supremacy doctrines of groups like the Ku Klux Klan. The reasoning goes like this: Individualism and merit-based systems of promotion do not lead to equal outcomes between groups. Thus, they are systems that enable racial inequity, which the CRT proponents then label "discrimination."

This is a recent statement from one of the most popular proponents of CRT, Ibram X. Kendi: "The most threatening racist movement is not the alt right's unlikely drive for a White ethnostate, but the regular American's drive for a 'race-neutral' one."[227]

It's important that people understand that Kendi is identifying great figures like Martin Luther King, Jr.'s campaign for a color-blind society as being the most threatening racist movement in the country. I challenge you to read Kendi's statement in any other way. Somehow, if we see each other as individuals, rather than as members of a certain racial or ethnic group, we're being racist. Let's look at a statement from Brittney Cooper, a tenured professor at Rutgers University's School of Arts and Sciences:

> I think it's a question that we should ask ourselves more often. Like, what do we believe about racism: do we think that it's actually a thing that can be conquered? Do we imagine a world in which it doesn't exist? Or do we, like many critical race theorists, say: this country was built on racism, racism is going to exist as long as America exists. And so, knowing that then how do we sort of, you know, situate our struggle? And so that is like one of the core questions, whenever I teach Critical Race Theory in my college classrooms, that I try to have with students.[228]

Let's simplify this statement down to what it really means. Martin Luther King, Jr., from his position as a minister of God, believed that if he appealed to the better angels of people's nature, if he could make the injustice visible, that people would change. Cooper questions whether that belief is true.

Perhaps that question is the heart of our dilemma, beyond any question of racism or bias.

When people are made aware of injustice, in whatever form that might take, can they be counted on to take the appropriate action? If they can, then our job is to highlight the inequities, as many civil rights leaders did, and trust that people will come to the proper conclusions. The goal of the critical race theorists, however, is to destroy racism and anything they see associated with it—primarily America and its culture.

If we do not believe that people can be trusted to come to the proper conclusions, then our only choice—if we wish to change things—will be to force it upon people, and in the process, create a tyranny worse than any preceding it.

>«

Who are some of the key founding players of CRT? Here are three of the best-known and influential advocates.

Derrick Bell. Bell is the author of two critical legal essays, "Serving Two Masters: Integration Ideals and Client Interests in School Desegregation Litigation"[229] and "Brown v. Board of Education: The Interest-Convergence Dilemma,"[230] and creator of the Harvard Law course "Race, Racism, and American Law," and is credited in a 2021 *New Yorker* article as being "The Man Behind Critical Race Theory."[231] In that course at Harvard, he taught the history of American law through the lens of race and power. Bell's ideological framework was rooted in Black nationalism and takes aim at the way racism permeates the judicial system. Bell believed that integration was *not* in the best interest of the African-American community, and that instead, the civil rights effort should have been focused on improving the outcomes of Black-only schools.

Following his departure from Harvard, Bell went on to become dean of the University of Oregon School of Law.

Kimberlé Crenshaw. Crenshaw was a student of Derrick Bell's at Harvard and has become his best-known acolyte. When Bell left Harvard to become dean at the University of Oregon School of Law, she helped to create an alternative course to Bell's, "Race, Racism, and American Law," which ensured that Bell's ideas remained part of the Harvard curriculum. Crenshaw is also credited with creating the term "intersectionality" in her 1989 paper "Demarginalizing the Intersection of Race and Sex: A Black Feminist Critique of Antidiscrimination, Doctrine, Feminist Theory and Antiracist Politics."[232] Let's explore how this works:

A straight Black man is oppressed because "Black" is a marginalized identity. However, a gay Black man has even less privilege because "gay" and "Black" together create an even more marginalized life experience in the CRT worldview. To go even further, to be Black and transgender is to be even more oppressed (least privileged) than either previous category due to the perceived low status of "transgender" in America.

Incentivizing oppression, that'll help foster strong people.

In a 2015 opinion piece in *The Washington Post*, Crenshaw continued her crusade for intersectionality:

> Intersectionality is an analytic sensibility, a way of thinking about identity and its relationship to power. Originally articulated on behalf of black women, the term brought to light the invisibility of many constituents within groups that claim them as members, but often fail to represent them. Intersectional erasures are not exclusive to black women. People of color within LGBTQ movements; girls of color in the fight against the school-to-prison pipeline; women within immigration movements; trans women within feminist movements; and people with disabilities fighting police abuse—all face vulnerabilities that reflect the intersections of racism, sexism, class oppression, transphobia, able-ism and more. Intersectionality has

given many advocates a way to frame their circumstances and fight for their visibility and inclusion.[233]

Ibram X. Kendi. Kendi is founding director of the Antiracist Research and Policy Center at American University in Washington, D.C., columnist for *The Atlantic*, and author of *The Beginning: The Definitive History of Racist Idea in America* and *How to Be an Antiracist*.[234] Kendi is a *New York Times* bestselling author and one of the most cited public speakers on racism.

What is "anti-racism"? To the average person, it sounds like it would mean "to be against discrimination, based on race or ethnicity." Most Americans are not racist people, and do not encourage discrimination. This is not the woke or progressive definition of "anti-racism"; in fact it's the complete antithesis. Here are some excerpts from Kendi's *How to Be an Antiracist*:

> **Antiracist:** One who is expressing the idea that racial groups are equals and none needs developing, and is supporting policy that reduces racial inequity.[235]

> The only remedy to racist discrimination is antiracist discrimination. The only remedy to past discrimination is present discrimination. The only remedy to present discrimination is future discrimination.[236]

> Intersectional Black identities are subjected to what Crenshaw described as the intersection of racism and other forms of bigotry, such as ethnocentrism, colorism, sexism, homophobia, and transphobia. My journey to being an antiracist first recognized the intersectionality of my ethnic racism, and then my bodily racism, and then my cultural racism, and then my color racism, and then my class racism, and, when I entered graduate school, my gender racism and queer racism.[237]

Intersectionality is the bedrock on which CRT is built. The intersectional approach of crossing identity groups to map oppression levels, combined with the "antiracist" philosophy of encouraging discrimination—if it were advertised honestly, surely far fewer Americans would be on board with implementing it.

»«

What is the actual value of diversity?

It is a genuinely important question and worthy of our time, given how often it is claimed to be our strength without a whisper of evidence to support it.

In the best of all possible worlds, a variety of people are brought together to work on an issue. They bring with them a variety of perspectives, ideas, and life experiences which may be helpful in solving the problem.

Through collaboration, discussion, debate, and compromise the group is more likely to develop an optimal solution that works for the greatest number of people with the fewest drawbacks.

The foundation of the idea is sound. The basis of the Socratic method; questioning different concepts, highlighting differences and similarities to determine the best course of action can only occur if there are different viewpoints at the start of the discussion. A similar truth pertains to competition, where those of similar skills compete to hone those skills. These clashes are not just beneficial for the winners; for those exposed to others performing at an even higher level, it can serve as a spur to further actions, such as additional effort, or a change in strategy.

However, in order to reap the benefits of diversity, the differences in perspectives and experiences must both be present. It's only because a diverse group can look at a problem from various angles that the best solution can be found. Getting a blonde, brunette, redhead, and a bald person together to solve a problem, who all come from the same background, attended the same college with the same major, is not likely to create a group with significant varying perspectives. That kind of diversity is only skin deep, and much of our media and culture is concentrating far too much on "visual diversity" rather than on actual diversity, as this CNN story from 2017:

> It was sparked by a recent White House photo op, when [President] Trump gathered with Republican leaders to celebrate the House passing a bill to repeal and replace Obamacare.
>
> The event looked like the board meeting of an all-white male golf club. Photos from the ceremony showed a phalanx of middle-aged white men heartily congratulating one another, with no woman or person of color in sight.
>
> Some photos released later did show some women at the event. But the surplus of white testosterone in the images sparked widespread outrage. One critic tweeted: "Message from another white guy: Yes, this is way too many white men in one place." Another white guy complained about a pattern of "overwhelming white maleness" on Trump administration photos. Someone even started a hashtag: #governmentsowhite.[238]

This simplistic view does not get to the core of the question of "What is the value of diversity?".

The hypothesis is that if a group is predetermined to have racial and gender diversity, then the group will have a variety of drastically lived experiences as a result, which will result in ideological diversity which can best address the problem.

The premise that simply because people have different racial identities, they automatically experience the world in drastically different ways is unsound. In fact, I find such a belief in itself to be racist. It is presuming to know the life circumstances of different people and judging them based on the pigment of their skin rather than on their individual actions and character, as Martin Luther King, Jr. urged us to do.

However, this belief, that color and what's between your legs determines how you think, is at the heart of intersectionality and CRT. Let's look at part of Dr. King's famous "I Have a Dream" speech:

> I still have a dream. It is a dream deeply rooted in the American dream. I have a dream that one day this nation will rise up and live out the true meaning of its creed. We hold these truths to be self-evident that all men are created equal.

> I have a dream that one day out in the red hills of Georgia the sons of former slaves and the sons of former slaveowners will be able to sit down together at the table of brotherhood...

> I have a dream that my four children will one day live in a nation where they will not be judged by the color of their skin but by the content of their character.[239]

Millions of Americans feel the same way. If slavery is the original sin of the United States, then it is Dr. King's formulation—rooted in our founding values—which gives us grace. One of the great strengths of America is that Americans are a future-oriented people. It doesn't mean that we don't consider the past, but that we are not bound by it.

If you go beyond American history and look at world history, you will find an amazing catalog of atrocities. The practice of slavery is not unique to, nor was it created in, early Colonial America. Europeans have butchered and enslaved other Europeans. Africans have butchered other Africans, as well as selling them into slavery. Asians have freely butchered other Asians, just look at what Mao did in China during the Great Leap Forward.

One of the brilliant ideas put forward by the Founding Fathers is that human beings, regardless of their good intentions, shouldn't have unchecked power. What better defense could there be against wholesale injustice against certain groups than to teach people not to look at people as groups, but as individuals?

For example, would you expect a Black man born and raised in New York City to have the same outlook as a Black man born and raised in rural Texas? How about a third-generation Cuban-American woman living in San Francisco and a Cuban-American woman who recently immigrated and lives in Miami?

Americans of all creeds and ethnicities fought together for decades to bring an end to racial discrimination, culminating in the 1964 Civil Rights Act under President Johnson. In 2023, it is fairly commonplace to see corporations and powerful institutions prioritizing positive racial discrimination, even in situations where it doesn't make any sense. Consider this 2018 article from the *Harvard Business Review* titled "Making U.S. Fire Departments More Diverse and Inclusive":

> Picture a typical firefighter. Who comes to mind? If you imagined a white man, that's understandable: 96% of U.S. career firefighters are men, and 82% are white. This homogeneity is striking, especially when you compare it to the U.S. military, which is 85% men and 60% white, and local police forces which are 88% men and 73% white. Many fire departments recognize that their lack of diversity is a problem and say they're committed to increasing racial and gender diversity.[240]

When did American diversity come to mean only diversity of appearance? One could think it arose naturally as an overcorrection from genuine racial discrimination in our past, which prevented Black Americans and other minority groups from attaining professional success in many fields. Perhaps a once well-meaning aim has become twisted through ideological fervor. But if so, then it is still our responsibility to fix the problem.

It is interesting to note how far things have come in such a relatively short period of time, specifically from the long-ago year of

2011 when our country was led by our first Black President, Barack Obama. This is taken directly from President Obama's Executive Order 13583:

> Our Nation derives strength from the diversity of its population and from its commitment to equal opportunity for all. We are at our best when we draw on the talents of all parts of society, and our greatest accomplishments are achieved when diverse perspectives are brought to bear to overcome our greatest challenges.
>
> A commitment to equal opportunity, diversity, and inclusion is critical for the Federal Government as an employer. By law, the Federal Government's recruitment policies should "endeavor to achieve a work force from all segments of society." (5 U.S.C. 2301(b)(1)). As the Nation's largest employer, the Federal Government has a special obligation to lead by example. Attaining a diverse, qualified workforce is one of the cornerstones of the merit-based service.[241]

The words of this 2011 executive order demonstrate how recently the belief that a difference in "perspectives" was the proper way to think about diversity. I will defend to the death the principle that people from all backgrounds and ethnicities should have the ability to work, compete, and advance based on their merit.

However, in the time since President Obama's executive order, the ideal of "diverse perspectives" has quickly twisted into diversity of race or gender, without regard to perspectives or experiences. Just ten years later, President Joe Biden's Administration announced:

> Today, the White House Office of Presidential personnel is releasing new data about the historic number and diversity of presidential appointees hired by Day 100 of the Biden-Harris Administration....

Many of these Administration leaders have broken new ground. Lloyd Austin is the first Black Secretary of Defense. Janet Yellen is the first woman to be Secretary of the Treasury. Alejandro Mayorkas is the first Latino to serve as Secretary of Health and Human Services. Deb Haaland, the Secretary of the Interior, is the first Native American to ever serve as a Cabinet Secretary. Pete Buttigieg is the first openly LGBTQ person to serve in the Cabinet. Cecilia Rouse is the first woman of color to chair the Council of Economic Advisers and Katherine Tai is the first woman of color to serve as U.S. Trade Representative.[242]

The result of this focus on skin color and gender not only minimizes these accomplished individuals as little more than tokens to represent a racial demographic, but it also reintroduces discrimination and barriers to progress based on race or gender. In the long term it will lead to a loss of genuine varied perspectives, and instead create ideological uniformity among groups, which will make them less productive.

What are we to make of these two wildly different views of diversity, propagated not by Republicans, but by two different Democratic Administrations? Are we allowed to have a civil discussion about differences between various groups?

The evidence and Big Tech suggest that we are not.

»«

In 2017, an engineer at Google named James Damore wrote a letter to his tech-giant employer, seeking to address what he saw as Google's ideological conformity and echo-chamber culture.

The letter began by explaining his view that this bias equated "freedom from offense" to "psychological safety" and as a consequence had silenced views that could be seen as offensive by some.[243] The result was a space where some ideas became immune from criticism, and among these ideas was the belief that "all disparities in discrimination are due to oppression" and that "discrimination should be used to correct the oppression."

Damore went onto explain that because of the company's unwillingness to address its own Left-leaning bias, it was also unwilling to address the contrasting view that "some disparity is due to factors other than oppression." As an example, he presented evidence that at least some of the gender gap in technology is explained by the *average* observed differences between men and women. Some of these differences included:

- Men on average have a higher drive for status; women on average prefer a more favorable work-life balance.
- Men on average are more competitive; women on average are more cooperative.
- Women on average show higher interest in people; men on average show higher interest in things.[244]

Damore then suggested some non-discriminatory methods to make the workplace more inclusive for women and explained some of the drawbacks of relying on discrimination to address the gender disparity. He also suggested that Google should stop alienating the views of conservatives, as their perspective was valuable and likely to be critical for continued profitability.

In an all-too-common pattern, the company did not respond by addressing Damore's arguments, but fired him for "perpetuating gender stereotypes."[245]

A similar chain of events took place at tech giant Apple in 2017, when the new vice president of Diversity and Inclusion, Denise Young Smith, a Black woman, wandered off the woke reservation. Here are her offending words:

> Diversity is the human experience. I get a little bit frustrated when diversity or the term diversity is tagged to people of color, or the women, or the LGBT.... There can be 12 white, blue-eyed, blond men in a

room and they're going to be diverse because they're going to bring a different life experience and life perspective to the conversation.[246]

Are you surprised that there was backlash over her comments and in predictable fashion she was forced to resign? Apparently, Apple doesn't believe that people who look the same can have different ideas.

These are organizations tasked with disseminating and distributing information. Google has the power to stop news, media, and factual information from reaching potentially billions of people. Apple has similar levels of influence in deciding what can go on iTunes or its app store.

If or—more accurately—when, these organizations decide that they no longer value diversity of thought, what implications does that have for the rest of us?

>«

Equity is just another word for discrimination.

Is that too bold of a statement to make?

I think it's justified. Follow my thinking: Most CRT advocates will say that equity is prioritizing the outcome for certain predetermined groups, rather than the opportunity to excel in those areas. In other words, it's like deciding which baseball team should win based on the ethnic or other diversity of the team rather than the players' ability. Why would anybody even show up to watch (or play, for that matter), if the outcome was already predetermined?

Here's a bold statement for you to chew on from Ibram X. Kendi. One might ask whether it was a good investment for the University of Virginia to pay him $32,500 for a speech—a little more than $500 a minute.[247] The Daily Wire has reported that the Boston University professor has raked in more than $300,000 in speaking fees through the end of 2020.[248] Here is some of Kendi's homespun wisdom: "If discrimination is creating equity, then it is antiracist. If discrimination is creating inequity, then it is racist."[249]

One might just as easily refer to this as the "I'm pro-discrimination" approach. That would probably take him all of six seconds to say, so maybe we should characterize that as fifty dollars of wisdom from Professor Kendi. However, this attack on equality of opportunity continues unabated as shown in this Vox article from 2015:

> Equality of opportunity is also a morally heinous idea. It is a way for us to justify the abandonment of people who—we insist—were given opportunities and squandered them. Even if it were possible to achieve equality of opportunity, it's not an achievement worth fighting for....
>
> Equal opportunity is nearly impossible to measure, but you know what we do know how to measure? If people's incomes are growing. How equal the income—and the wealth distribution is.[250]

The difficulty with many of these arguments is that they often start with a point or fact that might have wide agreement—and then veers into insanity. The lessons being learned by the young today are not that their choices can make them powerful, but that the machinations of others will keep them forever weak, no matter what they do. And that a powerful, overarching state is needed to correct the nebulous problem.

Maybe it's just a philosophical conceit with me, or even a "bias," but I genuinely believe that people can take actions to improve their lives, whatever that might mean to them.

Unfortunately, this is how the Biden Administration has taken the traditional idea of civil rights and inverted every one of its principles:

> Equal opportunity is the bedrock of American democracy, and our diversity is one of our country's greatest strengths. But for too many, the American Dream remains out of reach....

It is therefore the policy of my Administration that the Federal Government should pursue a comprehensive approach to advancing equity for all, including people of color and others who have been historically underserved, marginalized, and adversely affected by persistent poverty and inequality. Affirmatively advancing equity, civil rights, racial justice, and equal opportunity is the responsibility of the Whole of our government.[251] —Executive Order, 2021.

In modern discussions the terms "equality" and "equity" are often used interchangeably. However, I think it's important that we define our terms, so instead of my pronouns, let me give you my definitions:

Equality (of Opportunity): Removing structural or systematic barriers that impede an individual's ability to function at a basic level in society; where they are freely able to take opportunities to advance themselves if they succeed. Simply put: being able to participate freely in society, whether that means succeeding spectacularly or failing miserably, depending on my own actions. This is the idea of meritocracy, which I consider to be one of America's great contributions to the world.

Equity (of Outcome): Ensuring that identity groups have equivalent amounts of power, resources, and influence; generally advocated from a desire to address historic discrimination, generational poverty, or marginalized status. Simply put: advancing some identity groups over others in order to achieve economic parity or "fairness" among identity groups.

The meritocratic system itself is imperiled by the equity-of-outcome doctrine. A meritocracy depends on individuals reaping the rewards or consequences of their actions. The system must treat them as individuals above all else.

This is not a naive appeal to an ideal state of things. The meritocratic nature of America has been the result of a hard-fought battle against the wickedest aspects of human nature. The centuries of slavery and segregation prevented individuals from being able to access many jobs, professions, or even to attain their dignity. In some cases, executive action was vital in combatting such discrimination and providing equal opportunities for all people.

One of the shining examples from American history of this effort was Executive Order 8802, signed by President Franklin Roosevelt in 1941, which forced the end of racial discrimination in the national defense industry:

> Whereas there is evidence that available and needed workers have been barred from employment in industries engaged in defense production solely because of considerations of race, creed, color, or national origin, to the detriment of workers' morale, and of national unity.
>
> NOW, THEREFORE, by virtue of the authority vested in me by the Constitution and the statutes, and as a prerequisite to the successful conduct of our national defense production effort, I do hereby reaffirm the policy of the United States that there shall be no discrimination in the employment of workers in defense industries or government because of race, creed, color, or national origin...[252]

How, as an American, can I not be proud of President Roosevelt's action? It was exactly the step that needed to be taken, just as President Harry Truman did in 1948, integrating the military through Executive Order 9981:

> It is hereby declared to be the policy of the President that there shall be equality of treatment and opportunity in the armed services without regard to race, color, religion or national origin. This policy shall be put into effect as rapidly as possible, having due regard to the time required to effectuate any necessary changes without impairing efficiency or morale.[253]

How can any American today not be in favor of equality of treatment and opportunity?

Well, apparently Harry Truman would fall afoul of today's activists. He would be forced to pledge allegiance to equity. I have a suspicion that if such a demand was placed on President Truman, he'd let loose with one of his colorful epithets.

As American culture has become more influenced by the tenants of progressivism, intersectionality, and CRT, the belief in opportunity and equal treatment has slowly eroded in favor of this demand for equity. The reasons behind this shift stem from the core intersectional belief that any difference in outcome is primarily due to discrimination on the basis of identity. From the perspective of a critical race theorist, any system that does not actively discriminate and contribute to equity between racial identity groups is racist. And using the same logic, critical race theorists also believe that any system that is not actively contributing to equity between the genders is sexist. Just for good measure, if we're not also balancing different sexualities, then we're homophobic, as well.

Equity, or equality of outcome, requires active and continuous discrimination against individuals if it is to survive. If individuals of similar standing are free to choose their life paths according to their own desires, they will often arrive at different ends according to their choices. This will hold true for individuals within similar racial, gender, or cultural demographics, as well as for identical siblings raised under the same roof. Some people will choose to become doctors, engineers, mothers, fathers, entrepreneurs, or artists, because they have the freedom to pursue their own version of happiness. The result will be a difference in wealth, power, and resources among individuals and their identity groups, thus creating some form of inequity.

But if we're all pursuing what we want thanks to equality of opportunity, what's the problem? Some people may be satisfied with a Honda; to others, the symbol of success is a Tesla or Lamborghini.

>><<

In order to sustain a system of equity of outcome, another philosophical principle must accompany it: the soft bigotry of low expectations.

When you treat people as equals, you allow them to learn, grow, fail, and develop at similar levels. What happens if you teach a group of people that they cannot succeed without special intervention? What happens when you demand that the bar for access be lowered in order for some groups to obtain an equitable outcome?

These insane policies are now being enacted in the real world.

In 2021, Oregon governor Kate Brown signed SB 0744, a bill which suspended the requirement for students to show competence in "essential learning skills," such as math, reading, or writing to graduate.[254] The reason given by the governor's spokesman, Charles Boyle, was that the new policy would primarily benefit "Oregon's Black, Latino, Latinx, Indigenous, Asian, Pacific Islander, Tribal, and students of color." Boyle continued by explaining that, "Leaders from those communities have advocated time and again for equitable graduation standards, along with expanded learning opportunities and supports."[255]

One must wonder how one goes from "expanded learning opportunities and supports" (which might be a good thing based on economic circumstances) to not being required to show competence in "essential learning skills." Educators who do not want to create educated students are as useful as firemen who douse flames with gasoline, and perhaps equally as dangerous.

It's good to know there are still dissenting views. A case in point was Oregon Republican Representative Christine Drazan, who provided a more balanced discussion of the issue. She doubted the usefulness of standardized testing but argued that the proposed solution of suspending competence in essential skills would end up bringing further harm to students in the long term. A diploma was supposed to be an acknowledgment that a student had reached a basic level of competence in the required subjects. She went on to argue that a diploma is not intended for those who are often absent or refuse participation or cannot show the required level of proficiency.[256] I'm the first to agree that people can become successful without a diploma, but it should mean something. At the very least, a diploma gives schools, parents, and potential employers some guarantee that a certain level of competence had been attained. Think of the effect on teachers. This law removes accountability from the teachers for teaching the students. And what about the students short-changed by this situation? Schools are supposed to provide students with the skills they will need for a job and career.

And the craziness isn't just limited to the schools. It's infecting the rest of society.

In Washington State, the legislature proposed HB 1692—named Promoting Racial Equity in the Criminal Legal System by Eliminating Drive-By Shooting as a Basis for Elevating Murder in the First Degree to Aggravated Murder in the First Degree.[257] Think of the terror in which urban neighborhoods already live under the threat of gang violence, often delivered in the form of a drive-by shooting. The elevation of this crime to Aggravated Murder in the First Degree was obviously designed to reduce the likelihood of drive-by shootings by gang members.

But with this measure the state legislature was prioritizing the future of drive-by gang bangers over the law-abiding citizens of these communities. The co-author of this bill, Tarra Simmons, stated that the existing penalties for the law predominantly targeted gangs of young, Black people. The bill came at a time when the homicides in Washington had increased by 46 percent, of which 55 percent were Black victims.

Continuing the craziness of the West Coast, we move along to California. Proposition 16 was intended to repeal Amendment 209 of California's state constitution, which prohibited the state from discriminating in employment based on race, color, sex, ethnicity, or national origin.[258] Proposition 16 was designed to allow the government to discriminate based on a person's immutable characteristics—an idea that the majority of Californians defeated at the ballot box in 2020.

I bet that Dr. Martin Luther King, Jr. would have wept that Democrats wanted to repeal the following provisions of Section 31 of Proposition 209:

a) The state shall not discriminate against, or grant preferential treatment to, any individual or group on the basis of race, sex, color, ethnicity, or national origin in the operation of public employment, public education, or public contracting.

b) For the purposes of this section, "state" shall include, but not necessarily be limited to, the state itself, any city, county, city and county, public university system, including the University of California, community college district, school district, special district, or any other political subdivision or governmental instrumentality of or within the state.[259]

The proponents of Proposition 16 argued that certain identity groups had historically been barred from certain professions and opportunities, and that "race-neutral" policies had not brought about the necessary progress. Therefore, progressives are increasingly becoming comfortable with the idea of allowing the state to consider race and gender when hiring as a tool to redistribute the fruits of government contracts in an attempt to rebalance society.

It's remarkable that these progressive activists, who would probably say that they agree with Martin Luther King, Jr. if asked, are now engaged in tearing down that legacy. This is from Eva Paterson, president of the Equal Justice Society, urging Californians to support the dismantling of American racial colorblindness:

> People of color are treated differently. One way that people can act on their desire to eliminate systematic racism is to vote for Proposition 16. It gives people of color, and women, more power, more money. If you have more money, you have more access, more clout in the political system.[260]

This mindset aligns perfectly with Marxist ideals, as noted by one critic of the bill, Haibo Huang, co-founder of San Diego Asian Americans for Equality:

> Judging people by their skin color is morally repugnant. Equal opportunity is referenced to individual merits, it never guarantees equal results. To the contrary, enforcing equal outcome regardless of qualification and effort bears the hallmark of communism.[261]

In March 2021, the Biden Administration passed the American Rescue Plan Act of 2021.[262] The act was passed only with the tie-breaking vote of Vice President Kamala Harris herself. As part of the package, a Harm Reduction Program aimed to work under guidance from the Centers for Disease Control and Prevention to give priority to "underserved communities that are greatly impacted by substance use disorders."[263] According to Executive Order 13985, "Advancing Racial Equity and Support for Underserved Communities Through the Federal Government," an underserved community is defined as consisting of or including "Black, Latino, and Indigenous and Native American persons, Asian Americans and Pacific Islanders and other persons of color; members of religious minorities; lesbian, gay, bisexual, transgender, and queer (LGBTQ+) persons."[264]

The efforts give the appearance of wanting to help those populations who suffer from higher-than-expected levels of overdoses and diseases related to substance abuse. However, the plan is to distribute "safe smoking supplies/kits" and syringes to prevent the transmission of disease through the sharing of drug paraphernalia—something that the White House denied.[265]

It would be considered insanity to pretend to assist a struggling alcoholic by giving him a set of shot glasses. Encouraging the bad behavior at the root of the problem is not a strategy for success. The only thing it does is to provide politicians with the opportunity to "virtue signal" their supposed care for minority communities.

When you lower or eliminate the requirements for a group of people to achieve success, how is that going to help people? You are not providing a roadmap for their eventual independence, but simply making their dependence a little less onerous.

I cannot see this effort to provide drugs and drug paraphernalia to addicts as anything other than an attempt to destroy these communities. This approach is analogous to the attacks on police, because when police lower their vigilance in crime-ridden neighborhoods, the only thing that happens is the criminals become emboldened.

If you reduce the police presence in a wealthy neighborhood, say, Martha's Vineyard or Aspen, there won't be much difference.

Do the same thing in Detroit, Los Angeles, San Francisco, or Washington, D.C., and you have the makings of a disaster, entirely by human machinations.

>«

There is one final component of the ideology that plagues Western culture: propaganda. It is not only used by activists and radicals to spread their ideas, but it also results in the reshaping of the ideology itself as it is spread and often forced on the masses.

As more people and institutions became captured by DEI, so, too, did the organizations through which we communicate and share ideas, such as Facebook, Twitter, Google, and its subsidiary YouTube. As James Damore noted at Google, the company culture had a left-wing bias and favored ideas such as "diversity" and "equity" with complete disregard of the employees' own ideological blind spots.

Twitter was also subject to this issue of overwhelming political bias and ideological capture, and as the platform became one of the main social hubs for casual and official communication, its ability to affect the flow of information also grew exponentially, as did the consequences of its bias. By 2021, the platform wielded enough influence to silence the sitting President of the United States over a left-wing lie.[266]

However, the ideology was not just based on CRT, intersectionality, queer theory, anti-racism, and LGBTQIA+ activism. As these topics entered mainstream political discourse, they were both intentionally and automatically fed into the algorithms that feed content back to users. These concepts—or at least a headline's understanding of them— became a rallying tool for progressive activists who aligned themselves with the Democratic Party. Similarly, the America First, Make America Great Again, faction of the cultural Right is using the Republican Party for a revitalization of liberty-minded American constitutionalism.

The ideals of the "liberal" Left do not align with its new radical bedfellows on anything more than surface level. The traditional root of liberalism is individual liberty, which is the opposite aim of the collectivist nature of race-based and gender-based identity politics and culture. Even so, the stock Democratic concerns, such as environmentalism and social programs, became ensnared with racial equity and transgender rights as social media simultaneously promoted and suppressed certain ideas on a loop.

The resulting phenomenon was a partially formed, ever-changing shell of an ideology, that shares and builds on shared words, with different understandings for each person. A shared vocabulary, with every person using different definitions: one activist may define "sex" as the physical manifestation of reproductive organs, while another may classify it as merely a legal term with no biological correlation. Articles with nonsensical titles, such as *Time* magazine's "There Is No Climate Justice Without Racial Justice"[267] feed into this, reinforcing a worldview that is meant to grab the most attention from an algorithm.

Without any core understanding of the root philosophies—in part due to the rapid and condensed nature of sharing information on most social media platforms combined with the fact that these topics were more likely to be promoted by the algorithm—a perverse incentive was born. Attention-grabbing, low-information posts supporting progressive causes were more easily shared with millions of people. In turn, users were rewarded with "likes," followers, subscribers, and shares—an extremely valuable currency to any aspiring content developer, influencer, or social personality.

On the other end of this spectrum, the ideas that did not align with the new composite ideology—such as meritocracy and color-blindness—were shunned and suppressed though the same systems, shielding the ideology and its followers from much-needed criticism and challenge under the guise of "safety." Anyone from an ordinary citizen to a sitting political figure was subject to this ideologically lopsided censorship.[268] This left the amorphous identity without anything to reign in its increasingly radical elements, with the only unifying component being a loose vocabulary and a desire to band together for political power. Colloquially called "wokeness" or "woke ideology," the terms refer to being "awakened" to the truth of the world, while, in fact, being more akin to viewing every situation through a narrow, distorted, and rainbow-colored kaleidoscope.

> Wokeness is the modern left-liberal culture, formulated by social media algorithms. It is characterized by cult-like adherence to liberal social orthodoxy. That's all it is. And the example of this is Ukraine. Why woke people support a war in Ukraine doesn't make sense; it doesn't follow any academic theories.
>
> Why is it that Hasan Piker will say "Here are these things that I believe: trans rights. And also, for war in Ukraine." What do these things have to do with each other? Why does this individual have no principles? He just follows the orthodoxy. -Tim Pool [269]

This increased valuation of these ideals did not occur organically—it was reinforced behind the scenes at some of these media conglomerates, often at the behest of government-aligned actors.

One revelation that was discovered was the involvement of many government intelligence agents in social media giants, such as Twitter, to the point that one journalist likened the involvement to be so extreme that Twitter was an enforcement arm for the state. With its newfound avenue to exertion of power, the government was effectively able to instruct the so-called private company to take down whatever the government wished.

The scope of this censorship ranged from jokes at the expense of high-ranking government officials to the banning of the Hunter Biden laptop story, which cast serious doubt on the qualification of former Vice President Joe Biden.[270] All of these actions served to construct an artificial view of reality, rooted not only in a porous value system based on identity, but also in falsely framed information because a large portion of people were denied the opportunity to see information naturally. This artificial view of reality divided Americans even further along ideological lines.

Combined with an "anti-misgendering policy" that criminalized referring to any trans-identifying person as his or her sex or a previous name, and a one-sided enforcement of policies against "harassment," the ultimate safe space was created. A space where sharing progressive tenants was not only protected speech, but it was encouraged and promoted. Without any checks or balances, these ideas spread and became more distorted and extreme over a few years' time, until the ideas were unrecognizable to most people who were considered left-wing only a few years prior.

The desire for a society without racism morphed into racially segregated, "anti-racist" practices.

Gay rights degenerated into kink pride and compulsory drag story hour.

Trans acceptance became child mutilation and castration.

Feminist ideals to advance equality for women has become advocacy for men displacing women in women's spaces.

And finally, the call for the proletariat to overthrow the bourgeoisie and capitalism in twentieth-century Europe has become a call for the oppressed target identities to liberate themselves from patriarchal, inequitable, heteronormative, White Western culture everywhere.

EPILOGUE

WHAT DOES GENUINE COURAGE LOOK LIKE?

On April 16, 1963, Martin Luther King, Jr. was confined to a Birmingham jail for participating in civil rights demonstrations. The next year he would win the Nobel Peace Prize.

But as he sat in that jail cell, receiving criticism from the leaders of other religious congregations for pushing too quickly for change, he decided to write a letter which has become known to history as the "Letter from Birmingham Jail."

We as Americans believe that we know Martin Luther King, Jr., and yet, what do we remember beyond a few sections of his "I Have a Dream" speech? His letter began:

> My Dear Fellow Clergymen,
>
> While confined here in the Birmingham city jail, I came across your recent statement calling my present activities "unwise and untimely." Seldom, if ever, do I pause to answer criticism of my work and ideas. If I sought to answer all the criticisms that cross my desk, my secretaries would be engaged in little else during

the course of the day, and I would have no time for constructive work. But since I feel that you are men of genuine good will and your criticisms are sincerely set forth, I want to try to answer your statement in what I hope will be patient and reasonable terms.[271]

If you were in jail, concerned about your safety, and receiving criticism from other church leaders, would you be so measured? I'd probably use profanity. But not Dr. King, as he continued to explain:

In any nonviolent campaign there are four basic steps: collection of the facts to determine whether injustices exist; negotiation; self-purification; and direct action. We have gone through all these steps in Birmingham. There can be no gainsaying the fact that racial injustice engulfs this community.

Birmingham is probably the most thoroughly segregated city in the United States. Its ugly record of police brutality is widely known. Negroes have experienced grossly unjust treatment in the courts. There have been more unsolved bombings of Negro homes and churches in Birmingham than in any city in this nation. These are the hard, brutal facts of the case. On the basis of these conditions Negro leaders sought to negotiate with the city fathers. But the latter consistently refused to engage in good faith negotiation.[272]

We do not have such heroism in America today, in part because we have no such system of oppression. Martin Luther King, Jr. won the battle for civil rights and we are the happy beneficiaries. And yet, even in the face of such hatred and violence, King's message was of love, recalling great figures of history who followed a similar path:

But as I continued to think about the matter I gradually gained a bit of satisfaction from being considered an extremist. Was not Jesus an extremist in love—"Love your enemies, bless them that curse you, pray for them that despitefully use you." Was not Amos an extremist for justice—"Let justice roll down like waters and righteousness like a mighty stream." Was not Paul an extremist for the gospel of Jesus Christ—"I bear in my body the marks of the Lord Jesus." Was not Martin Luther an extremist—"Here I stand: I can do none other so help me God." Was not John Bunyan an extremist—"I will stay in jail to the end of my days before I make a butchery of my conscience." Was not Abraham Lincoln an extremist—"This nation cannot survive half slave and half free." Was not Thomas Jefferson an extremist—"We hold these truths to be self-evident, that all men are created equal." So the question is not whether we will be extremists but what kind of extremists will we be? Will we be extremists for hate or will we be extremists for love? Will we be extremists for the cause of justice?[273]

What a wonderful thing to be an extremist for love and justice. That is the legacy that Martin Luther King, Jr. leaves us with, in perfect replication of the ideal taught to us by Jesus Christ. Martin Luther King, Jr. stands among the greatest Americans who helped to correct the course of the culture and move this country closer toward its founding ideals. He was also great because the humble gospel that he preached was one of love, justice, and humility.

In modern culture, it's very easy to be labeled an extremist. In my own experience, the mere act of criticizing child sex changes or condemning violent BLM and Antifa extremists for besieging American cities for weeks can earn you the label.

In November 2019, undercover journalist organization Project Veritas, under the leadership of American muckraker James O'Keefe, released one of the most damning stories in the history of the country.

In this expose, Amy Robach, an anchor for ABC News, was caught on a hidden mic discussing the fact that the studio was in possession of an unreleased documentary exposing the life of socialite Jeffrey Epstein, as well as his social ties to government actors and foreign royals, and even testimony from his victims:

> She [Virginia Roberts Giuffre] told me everything. She had pictures, she had everything. She was in hiding for 12 years. We convinced her to come out. We convinced her to talk to us. Um, it was unbelievable what we had Clinton [Bill], we had everything.
>
> I tried for three years to get it [the Epstein Story] on, to no avail. And now it's all coming out and it's like these new revelations and I freaking had all of it. I'm so pissed right now....
>
> There will come a day when we will realize Jeffrey Epstein was the most prolific pedophile this country has ever known....
>
> So do I think he was killed? 100% Yes, I do... He made his whole living blackmailing people... Yup, there were a lot of men in those planes. A lot of men who visited that island, a lot of powerful men who came into that apartment.[274]

This story was my first exposure to actual investigative journalism, the kind you see in stories where the hero always wins, and his exploits are chronicled in print and delivered by an over-eager paperboy on a bike.

The sheer courage to stand up and expose the most powerful and well-connected people in the world as they're committing the evilest of acts is nothing short of heroic. Not many possess that level of valor and fortitude needed to risk earning the ire of the ultra-elite criminal class. However, we all possess the ability to make changes in our own lives and spheres of influence, and we must not be afraid to stand up and do what's just.

The "anti-racist" activists preaching racial segregation are ideologically not much different from the racial supremacists of the Jim Crow era. The elite scum stalking children while visiting a billionaire's island are not much different from the hospitals and surgeons carving and scarring children's bodies for money and social influence.

This is unacceptable, illiberal, and fundamentally un-American and *must* be stopped.

We are currently in a war for America's culture. If we lose, the values of the following generations—and in turn, American culture itself—will be destroyed, and the rights, education, and futures of the new generations will be stolen. Americans must fight back and rebuild our culture and affirm our values, principles, and beliefs.

Teaching others, especially children, to view and judge others based on their race, sex, and sexuality will not create a world with less racism. It will create a world with more hate and division than ever before. Secretly converting workplaces and schools into ideological safe spaces only serves to prevent people from marginalized groups from integrating with their wider community, while not allowing them to learn and have their ideas challenged. Confused minors should not be allowed to have sex changes or sterilizing experimental surgeries.

Standing for your values, in the face of overwhelming dissent, is the essence of courage.

It is in that spirit that I and Kent Heckenlively thank you, dear reader, for the time you took to read this book. We hope that you will consider the arguments presented here.

...but wait, there's more.

THE NEWSPEAK DICTIONARY

The term Newspeak originates from George Orwell's iconic work *1984*, where it is the official language of the country Oceania. The core function of the language is to restrict the ability of the citizenry to express fundamental concepts, in order to manufacture and maintain the false worldview created by the totalitarian government:

> Countless other words such as honour, justice, morality, internationalism, democracy, science, and religion had simply ceased to exist. A few blanket words covered them, and, in covering them, abolished them. All words grouping themselves round the concepts of liberty and equality, for instance, were contained in the single word crimethink, while all words grouping themselves round the concepts of objectivity and rationalism were contained in the single word oldthink. Greater precision would have been dangerous.[275]

In modern cultural discourse, the two sides of the cultural divide do not speak the same language. Activists and academics have weaponized language in order to subvert culture and manipulate individuals to achieve their ideological ends. By understanding the language, genuine discussion and criticism can be fostered.

Term	Common English Meaning (What it actually means)	Newspeak Meaning (What the leftists say)
Accomplice	A more radical version of an ally.	A step beyond ally; someone who takes direct action for marginalized groups.
Ally	A person who acts on the behalf of an identity group without belonging to it.	Someone acknowledged by a member of a marginalized group as being an active advocate for said group.
Anti-Blackness	Attitudes that oppose "antiracism" and identity politics in favor of color-blindness and meritocracy.	Attitudes that acknowledge and support the idea that America is a racist system, which historically and currently oppresses non-Whites.
Antiracism	Supporting discrimination to achieve equality of outcome.	Supporting actions or policies that promote discrimination to achieve "equity."
Belonging	A sense of value and worth toward a particular group, without allowing criticism.	A sense of value and worth toward a particular group.
Blackness	Catch-all term for American Black culture or being Black in America; often used with the implications of "struggle" or African nationalism with some allegiance to progressive policies and causes.	The phenomenology or genealogy of being Black, or experiencing African or American Black culture, particularly Black urban culture.

Critical Race Theory	An ideology based on Marxism, splitting people into "oppressed" and "oppressor" classes, using race and sex instead of class to promote grievance and retribution politics.	A framework to address how race and power dynamics affect American law and culture.
Diversity	Varied group identities present, all members in agreement with the tenants of DEI.	A broad set of individuals from underrepresented or marginalized identity groups based on race, sex, sexuality, gender, and gender identity.
Equality	The opportunity for all to engage in an activity or pursuit, without enacting barriers for some to benefit others; "a level playing field."	A system that allows some to reach highs that others will not, resulting in disparity in the end result.
Equity	Forced reallocation of power and economic resources from individuals to benefit non-majority identity groups (equality of outcome).	Ensuring material and status equality across identity groups.
Gender	Biologically influenced habits, social dynamics, and expectations that are linked to one's biological sex.	Arbitrarily defined, socially constructed categories and expectations for the sexes.
Gender Expression	The degree to which someone appears masculine or feminine through clothing and mannerisms.	The outward manifestation of one's gender identity, generally through clothes, accessories, and behavior.

Gender Identity	The ideal image of oneself, possibly fantastical and unattached to any biological reality. Often conflated with "sex."	One's inner perception of who one is, without regard to biological sex. Fluid and subject to change at any time.
Inclusion	Creating ideological spaces that shield certain identity groups from criticism; adopting practices that prop up perceived identities over others.	Attitudes and practices that encourage and foster diversity and affirm marginalized individuals.
Intersectionality	A framework that recognizes group identity over the individual, and perceives all inequity between identities as the result of discrimination.	A framework that seeks to identify and address power imbalances between and across identity groups, such as race, sex, gender, ethnicity, and sexuality.
Man	Adult human male.	Anyone who identifies as such, regardless of biological sex. Fulfills the masculine role in society.
Microaggression	Any subtle interaction (or lack thereof) that can be interpreted as discriminatory based on race, sex, gender, religion, or any other identity.	The everyday, subtle interactions or behaviors that can communicate some sort of bias toward historically marginalized groups.
Racism	Discrimination based on race or ethnicity.	Discrimination enabled by power imbalances between Whites and non-Whites. "Power and prejudice."

Sex	The biological dichotomy between male and female, dictated by XX or XY chromosomes and the resulting primary reproductive systems. Often used interchangeably with "gender" and "gender identity."	The primary reproductive organs and associated hormones, arbitrarily assigned by doctors at birth with no biological basis or assumed impact on sexuality, or personality of the individual.
Sexism	Discrimination based on sexual category—male or female.	Discrimination enabled by power imbalances between men and women; advocate of policies promoting material equity between the sexes.
Sexuality	Direction of sexual attraction. Heterosexual, homosexual, or indifferent.	Level of attraction toward one or both sets of genitalia, possibly separate from the gender expression of the person.
Tolerance	Passive acceptance of something without agreement or condemnation.	Passive acceptance lacking endorsement, which doesn't foster positive emotion.
Transphobia	Discrimination based on transgender status.	Fear, hatred, discrimination, or critical attitudes toward trans-people, or policies that advantage trans-people.
Whiteness	Post-Enlightenment, individualist Western culture. Meritocracy, natural rights, and liberty.	Attitudes, decisions, and policies that support a "White dominant culture." Anything that results in inequity among races.

Wokeness / Woke Culture	Shallow amalgamation of cult-like allegiance to progressive ideologies, spread via social media algorithms. Often used pejoratively.	Advocate for environmental equity, LGBTQIA+ inclusion, racial justice, and antiracist practices. Social justice ally.[276]
Woman	1. Adult human female 2. See #1.	1. Anyone who identifies as such, regardless of perceived appearance or biological sex. 2. Someone who wants to identify with the physical characteristics and the social role of a female.

ENDNOTES

1. "Fact Sheet: 100 Days in, Biden-Harris Administration Makes History with Presidential Appointees," The White House, April 29, 2021, https://web.archive.org/web/20210429114753/https://www.whitehouse.gov/briefing-room/statements-releases/2021/04/29/fact-sheet-100-days-in-biden-harris-administration-makes-history-with-presidential-appointees/.

2. Peter Belfiore, "Oregon Scraps Math, English High School Graduation Requirements," MSN, *Daily Mail*, August 10, 2021, https://web.archive.org/web/20210811163529/https://www.msn.com/en-us/news/us/oregon-scraps-math-english-high-school-graduation-requirements/ar-AAN9Jku.

3. Travis Mitchell, "How Americans See the State of Race Relations," Pew Research Center's Social & Demographic Trends Project, Pew Research Center, September 22, 2021, https://www.pewresearch.org/social-trends/2019/04/09/how-americans-see-the-state-of-race-relations/.

4. Tori B. Powell, "45% Of LGBTQ Youth Seriously Considered Suicide in the Past Year, Trevor Project Survey Finds," CBS News CBS Interactive, May 4, 2022, https://www.cbsnews.com/news/lgbtq-youth-suicide-the-trevor-project-mental-health-2022/.

5. "See Color: The Crystal Gems Say Be Anti-Racist | Steven Universe| Cartoon Network," YouTube Video, Cartoon Network, 1:43, February 16, 2021, https://www.youtube.com/watch?v=zJkVgGYm4xo.

6. Justine Schober, M.D., "Lupron Sex Offender Therapy," Full Text View - ClinicalTrials.gov, September 22, 2005, https://clinicaltrials.gov/ct2/show/NCT00220350.

7. Juno Dawson and Spike Gerrell, "The Ins and Outs of Gay Sex," Essay in *This Book Is Gay*, (London, UK: Hot Key Books, 2020), 169–73.

8. Carl Benjamin and Peter Boghossian, "Kindly Inquisitors," YouTube Video, Portland State University, 1:26:21, June 2, 2018, https://www.youtube.com/watch?v=32voovwKxtA.

9. Kimberlé Crenshaw, "Demarginalizing the Intersection of Race and Sex: A Black Feminist Critique of Antidiscrimination Doctrine, Feminist Theory and Antiracist Policies," Internet Archive, University of Chicago Legal Forum, August 15, 2017, https://archive.org/details/DemarginalizingTheIntersectionOfRaceAndSexABlackFeminis.

10. Ibram X. Kendi, *How to Be an Antiracist* (New York, NY: One World, August 13, 2019), 188–89.

11. Ulysses Smith, "The What and Why of DEI," *Diversity, Equity, and Inclusion: A Beginner's Guide,"* Udemy, 2019, accessed July 21, 2022, www.udemy.com/course/diversity-equity-and-inclusion-a-beginners-guide/learn/lecture/16241954#content.

12. Ulysses Smith, "From Tolerance to Inclusion & Belonging," *Diversity, Equity and Inclusion: A Beginner's Guide,* Udemy, 2019, accessed July 21, 2022, www.udemy.com/course/diversity-equity-and-inclusion-a-beginners-guide/learn/lecture/16239594#learning-tools, www.udemy.com/course/diversity-equity-and-inclusion-a-beginners-guide/learn/lecture/16241978#content/.

13. Ibid., Ulysses Smith, "Exploring Equity and Equality," *Diversity, Equity and Inclusion: A Beginner's Guide,* Udemy, 2019, accessed July 21, 2022, www.udemy.com/course/diversity-equity-and-inclusion-a-beginners-guide/learn/lecture/16241982#content/.

14. Ibid.

15. Ibid.

16. Ibid.

17. Ibid.

18. Dame Vivian Hunt, Dennis Layton, and Sara Prince, "Why Diversity Matters," McKinsey & Company, January 1, 2015, www.mckinsey.com/capabilities/people-and-organizational-performance/our-insights/why-diversity-matters.

19. Ulysses Smith, "From Tolerance to Inclusion & Belonging," *Diversity, Equity and Inclusion: A Beginner's Guide,* Udemy, 2019, accessed July 21, 2022, www.udemy.com/course/diversity-equity-and-inclusion-a-beginners-guide/learn/lecture/16239594#learning-tools.

20. Ibid.

21. Ibid.

22. Ibid.

23. Ibid.

24. Ibid.

25. "GOP Rep. questions Biden official on Term 'Birthing Person,'" YouTube Video, 1:26, June 9, 2021, https://www.youtube.com/watch?v=54gyph5szdI.

26. Ibid.

27. Ibid.

28. Ibid.

29. Project Veritas, "Insider Leaks Critical Race Theory 'Indoctrination' Within Children's Toy Manufacturer Hasbro," YouTube Video, 27:18, July 18, 2021, https://www.youtube.com/watch?v=YwN8NFRLpo8.

30. Ibram X. Kendi, *How to Be an Antiracist* (New York, NY: One World, August 13, 2019), 186–87.

31. Alia E. Dastagir, "Marsha Blackburn asked Ketanji Brown Jackson to define 'Woman.' Science says there's no simple answer," *USA Today*, March 24, 2022, www.usatoday.com/story/life/health-wellness/2022/03/24/marsha-blackburn-asked-ketanji-jackson-define-woman-science/7152439001/.

32. Eric McDaneil, "The Senate Confirms Ketanji Brown Jackson to the Supreme Court," NPR, April 7, 2022, www.npr.org/2022/04/07/1090973786/ketanji-brown-jackson-first-black-woman-supreme-court.

33. Julie Beaulieu, "Gender and Sexuality: Diversity and Inclusion in the Workplace," University of Pittsburgh, www.coursera.org/learn/gender-sexuality?action=enroll.

34. Julie Beaulieu and Susan Marine, "About this Course" from "Gender and Sexuality: Diversity and Inclusion in the Workplace," University of Pittsburgh, https://www.coursera.org/learn/gender-sexuality/lecture/UtRp2/course-introduction.

35. Ibid.

36. Ibid.

37. Ibid.

38. Ibid.

39. Julie Beaulieu, "Sexuality" from "Gender and Sexuality: Diversity and Inclusion in the Workplace," University of Pittsburgh, accessed August 1, 2022, https://www.coursera.org/learn/gender-sexuality/lecture/gAy0Y/sexuality.

40. Ibid.

41. Ibid.

42. Ibid.

43. Susan Marine, "LGBTQIA Issues in the Workplace" from "Gender and Sexuality: Diversity and Inclusion in the Workplace," University of Pittsburgh, https://www.coursera.org/learn/gender-sexuality/lecture/WeESb/lgbtqia-issues-in-the-workplace.

44. Ibid.

45. Jordan Peterson, "The Gender Scandal: Part One (Scandinavia) and Part Two (Canada)," February 24, 2019, www.jordanbpeterson.com/political-correctness/the-gender-scandal-part-one-scandinavia-and-part-two-canada/.

46. Ibid.

47. Ibid.

48. Karin Agness Lips, "Men Work Longer Hours Than Women," *Forbes*, June 30, 2016, www.forbes.com/sites/karinagness/2016/06/30/new-report-men-work-longer-hours-than-women/?sh=3c1e136118b4.

49. Susan Marine, "LGBTQIA Issues in the Workplace" from "Gender and Sexuality: Diversity and Inclusion in the Workplace," University of Pittsburgh, https://www.coursera.org/learn/gender-sexuality/lecture/WeESb/lgbtqia-issues-in-the-workplace.

50. Julie Beaulieu, "Sexuality in Theory - the History of Sexuality and Sexuality in Theory" from "Gender and Sexuality: Diversity and Inclusion in the Workplace," University of Pittsburgh. https://www.coursera.org/learn/gender-sexuality/lecture/BdVnb/sexuality-in-theory.

51. Ibid.

52. Dominic Sandbrook, "Titan of Terror," *The Daily Mail*, May 5, 2018, https://www.dailymail.co.uk/news/article-5693381/Karl-Marx-titan-terror-communist-ideology-murdered-millions.html.

53. Ibid.

54. Kristen Altus, "Missouri AG Doubles down on Firing School Officials Who Took Students to Drag Show: 'It's a Huge Problem,'" *Fox Business*, February 1, 2023. https://www.foxbusiness.com/politics/missouri-ag-doubles-down-firing-school-officials-students-drag-show-huge-problem.

55. Patrick Miller and Keith Simon, "A Public School Took Middle Schoolers to a Drag Show Without Telling Their Parents," *Newsweek*, January 25, 2023. https://www.newsweek.com/public-school-district-took-middle-schoolers-drag-show-without-telling-their-parents-opinion-1776503.

56. Valerie Richardson, "New York mayor backs city-funded Drag Queen Story Hour for school children," *The Washington Times*, June 16, 2022. https://www.washingtontimes.com/news/2022/jun/16/eric-adams-throws-support-behind-drag-queen-story-/.

57. Ruben, Gayle S. "Thinking Sex: Notes for a Radical Theory of the Politics of Sexuality." The Middlebury Sites Network, 1984. https://web.archive.org/web/20230217180312/http://www.sites.middlebury.edu/sexandsociety/files/2015/01/rubin-thinking-sex.pdf.

58. Hoover Institution, "Facts and Fallacies with Thomas Sowell," YouTube Video,33:37, May 19, 2011, https://www.youtube.com/watch?v=V6ZPg6kOBkc.

59. Ibram X. Kendi, *How to Be an Antiracist* (New York, NY: One World, August 13, 2019), 25–26.

60. Ibid., 193–95.

61. Ibid., 20–21.

62. Christopher F. Rufo, "Woke Elementary," Christopher F. Rufo, Substack, January 13, 2021, https://christopherrufo.com/woke-elementary/.

63. Sue Rieke-Smith and Maureen Wolf, "Resolution 1920-19," Equity and Inclusion/Resolution/Resolución 1920-19, Tigard-Tualatin School District, June 8, 2020, https://web.archive.org/web/20210226063036/https://www.ttsdschools.org/Page/9770.

64. Christopher F. Rufo, "'Antiracism' Comes to the Heartland," Christopher F. Rufo, Substack, January 19, 2021, https://christopherrufo.com/antiracism-comes-to-the-heartland/.

65. "Talking About Race – Whiteness," Smithsonian National Museum of African American History and Culture," accessed October 25, 2022, www.nmaahc.si.edu/learn/talking-about-race/topics/whiteness.

66. Ibid.

67. Rudyard Kipling, "The White Man's Burden": Kipling's Hymn to U.S. Imperialism, "The White Man's Burden: The United States & The Philippine Islands, 1899," *Rudyard Kipling's Verse: Definitive Edition* (Garden City, New York: Doubleday, 1929), https://historymatters. gmu.edu/d/5478/.

68. Jacob McWilliams, PhD, "Queering the Schoolhouse: LGBTQ+ Inclusion for Educators," University of Colorado, 2020. https:// www.coursera.org/learn/queeringtheschoolhouse/lecture/wfNpe/ jacob-mcwilliams-phd.

69. Ibid., Daryl Boyd,https://www.coursera.org/learn/queeringtheschool house/lecture/P8Uxc/daryl-boyd.

70. Ibid., Suraj Uttamchandani, PhD, https://www.coursera.org/learn/ queeringtheschoolhouse/lecture/hgekq/suraj-uttamchandani-phd.

71. Ibid., McWilliams, Jacob, and Daryl Boyd, "Allyship, Accomplices, and Advocates," https://www.coursera.org/learn/queeringtheschoolhouse/ lecture/xrjBs/allyship-accomplices-and-advocates.

72. Barbara Dennis, Suraj Uttamchandani, Spencer Biery, and Aubrie Blauvelt. "LGBTQIA+ Youth as Multicultural Educators," *Ethnography and Education*, vol. 14, no. 3, February 12, 2019, 360–76. https://doi. org/10.1080/17457823.2019.1578983.

73. Suraj Uttamchandani, PhD, "History in Schools," in "Queering the Schoolhouse: LGBTQ+ Inclusion for Educators," University of Colorado, 2020, www.coursera.org/learn/queeringtheschoolhouse/ lecture/GUOIH/current-circumstances/.

74. Jacob McWilliams, Daryl Boyd, & Suraj Uttamchandani, "Queering the Schoolhouse: LGBTQ+ Inclusion for Educators," https://www. coursera.org/learn/queeringtheschoolhouse.

75. Ibid.

76. Ibid.

77. Lester, David. "Suicidal Behavior in African-American Slaves." OMEGA - Journal of Death and Dying 37, no. 1 (1998): 1–13. https://doi.org/10.2190/qx9p-68dp-hx8u-l4aa.

78. Richard Branstrom, PhD, and John E. Pachankis, PhD, "Reduction in Mental Health Treatment Utilization Among Transgendered Individuals After Gender-Affirming Surgeries: A Total Population Study," *American Journal of Psychiatry*, vol. 177, no. 8, (October 4, 2019): 727–34, www.doi.org/10.1176/appi.ajp.2019.19010080.

79. "A Guide to Supporting Lesbian, Gay, Bisexual, Transgender, and Queer Students in Your School," GLSEN, 2020, https://www.glsen.org/sites/default/files/2019-11/GLSEN%20English%20SafeSpace%20Book%20Text%20Updated%202019.pdf.

80. Ibid.

81. Ibid.

82. Laura Moorhead, "LGBTQ+ Visibility in the K-12 Curriculum," Kappan Online, September 24, 2018, https://kappanonline.org/moorhead-lgbtq-visibility-k-12-curriculum/.

83. Ibid.

84. Scott O. Lillienfeld and Hal Arkowitz, "Why 'Just Say No' Doesn't Work," *Scientific American MIND*, January 1, 2014, https://www.scientificamerican.com/article/why-just-say-no-doesnt-work/.

85. "What We Believe," Black Lives Matter, September 7, 2019, https://web.archive.org/web/20200917194804/https://blacklivesmatter.com/what-we-believe/.

86. Jennifer Kingson, "Exclusive: $1 Billion-Plus Riot Damage is Most Expensive in Insurance History," *Axios,* September 10, 2020, https://www.axios.com/2020/09/16/riots-cost-property-damage.

87. Lois Beckett, "At Least 25 Americans Were Killed During Protests and Political Unrest in 2020," *The Guardian*, October 31, 2020, www.theguardian.com/world/2020/oct/31/americans-killed-protests-political-unrest-acled

88. "Tides Foundation," Influence Watch, accessed September 29, 2022, www.influencewatch.org/non-profit/tides-foundation/.

89. Thousand Currents website homepage, accessed May 9, 2023. https://thousandcurrents.org/.

90. "Thousand Currents," Influence Watch, accessed September 29, 2022, www.influencewatch.org/non-profit/thousand-currents/.

91. Ibid.

92. "Tides Welcomes Black Lives Matter as a New Partner," *Perspective by Tides*, Tides Foundation, July 2, 2020, https://www.tides.org/our-community/partnerships/tides-welcomes-black-lives-matter/.

93. Hayden Ludwig, "Tides Center Takes Control of Black Lives Matters Global Network," July 28, 2020, Capital Research Organization, https://capitalresearch.org/article/tides-center-takes-control-of-black-lives-matter-global-network/.

94. Ibid.

95. Stephen Kinzer, *Poisoner in Chief: Sidney Gottlieb and the CIA Search for Mind Control*, (Henry Holt and Co., New York, September 10, 2019), 83–84.

96. Julia Layton & Alia Hoyt, "How Brainwashing Works," *How Stuff Works*, October 4, 2021, www.science.howstuffworks.com/life/inside-the-mind/human-brain/brainwashing.htm.

97. Ibid.

98. Ibid.

99. Ibid.

100. Adina Campbell, "What is Black Lives Matter and What are the Aims?" BBC, June 13, 2021, www.bbc.com/news/explainers-53337780.

101. Lizette Alvarez and Cara Buckley, "Zimmerman is Acquitted in Trayvon Martin Killing," *The New York Times*, July 13, 2013, www.nytimes.com/2013/07/14/us/george-zimmerman-verdict-trayvon-martin.html.

102. Katie Benner, "Eric Garner's Death Will Not Lead to Federal Charges for NYPD Officer," *The New York Times*, July, 16, 2019 www.nytimes.com/2019/07/16/nyregion/eric-garner-daniel-pantaleo.html.

103. Doha Madani, "Fired NYPD Officer in Eric Garner's Chokehold Death, Daniel Pentelo, Sues to Get His Job Back," NBC News, October 23, 2019, www.nbcnews.com/news/us-news/fired-nypd-officer-eric-garner-s-chokehold-death-daniel-pantaleo-n1071076.

104. John Eligon, "No Charges for Ferguson Officer who Killed Michael Brown, New Prosecutor Says," *The New York Times*, July 30, 2020,

www.nytimes.com/2020/07/30/us/michael-brown-darren-wilson-ferguson.html.

105. Jonathan Capehart, "'Hands up, Don't Shoot' was Built on a Lie," *The Washington Post*, March 16, 2015.

106. Amy Forliti, "Lawyers for ex-cops raise Floyd's history of crime, drug use," *Associated Press*, September 2020, www.apnews.com/article/trials-crime-minneapolis-racial-injustice-a7eaaa81fc7ed-31270f0aa342040e07b.

107. Ibid.

108. "Derek Chuavin Sentenced to 20 Years for Violating George Floyd's Civil Rights," *BBC*, July 7, 2020,www.bbc.com/news/world-us-canada-62088103.

109. Daniella Silva, "April 7 Highlights for the Murder Trial of Derek Chauvin Day 8." NBCNews.com. *NBC Universal News Group*, April 7, 2021. https://www.nbcnews.com/news/us-news/live-blog/derek-chauvin-trial-2021-04-07-n1263278/ncrd1263333#liveBlogCards.

110. Adina Campbell, "What is Black Lives Matter and what are the Aims?" BBC, June 13, 2021, www.bbc.com/news/explainers-53337780.

111. Annie E. Casey Foundation website, "About Us," accessed September 26, 2022, www.aecf.org.about.

112. Annie E. Casey Foundation, 990F (016), www.projects.propublica.org/nonprofits/organizations/521951681/201703189349102630/full

113. "About," Accountable Justice Action Fund, accessed September 26, 2022, www.accountablejusticeaction.org/

114. "Accountable Justice Action Fund." InfluenceWatch. Accessed August 13, 2023. https://www.influencewatch.org/non-profit/accountable-justice-action-fund/.

115. "About Us," The Bauman Family Foundation, accessed September 26, 2022, www.baumanfoundation.org/about-us/foundation.

116. Bauman Family Foundation Grants, accessed September 26, 2022, 20, www.baumanfoundation.org/grants/search/.

117. "Committed grants," Bill and Melinda Gates Foundation, accessed September 26, 2022, www.gatesfoundation.org/about/committed-grants?q=tides.

118. "Grants Database," Carnegie Corporation of New York, accessed September 26, 2022, www.carnegie.org/grants/grants-database/grantee/tides-center/#!/grants/grants-database/grant/531406801.0/.

119. "Grants and Mission Investments," David and Lucile Packard Foundation, accessed September 26, 2022, www.packard.org/grants-and-investments/grants-database/.

120. "Grants Database," The Ford Foundation, accessed September 26, 2022, www.fordfoundation.org/work/our-grants/grants-database/grants-all/.

121. "Awarded Grants," Open Society Foundations, founded by George Soros, accessed September 27, 2022, www.opensocietyfoundations.org/grants/past.

122. "Grants," Jennifer and Jonathon Allan Soros Foundation, accessed September 27, 2022, "Jennifer and Jonathan Allan Soros Foundation." InfluenceWatch, June 25, 2021. https://www.influencewatch.org/non-profit/jennifer-and-jonathan-allan-soros-foundation/.

123. Influence Watch, accessed September 27, 2022, www.influencewatch.org/non-profit/tides-foundation/.

124. "Grants Search," John D. and Catherine T. MacArthur Foundation, accessed September 27, 2022, www.macfound.org/grants/.

125. Influence Watch, accessed September 27, 2022, www.influencewatch.org/non-profit/tides-foundation/.

126. "Grant database," Oak Fund, accessed September 27, 2022, www.oakfnd.org/grants/.

127. Omidyar Network Fund, accessed September 27, 2022, www.omidyar.com/wp-content/uploads/2020/09/ONFI-2017-990-PF.pdf.

128. Robert Wood Johnson Foundation, accessed September 27, 2022, www.rwjf.org/en/how-we-work/grants.

129. "Grants search," Rockefeller Brothers Fund, accessed September 27, 2022, www.rbf.org/grants.

130. Influence Watch, accessed September 27, 2022, www.influencewatch.org/non-profit/tides-foundation/.

131. Influence Watch, accessed October 3, 2022, www.influencewatch.org/non-profit/tides-foundation/, (Keywords: "Rockefeller Philanthropic Advisors").

132. "Grants Database," Ford Foundation, accessed November 26, 2022, https://www.fordfoundation.org/work/our-grants/grants-database/.

133. "Tides Foundation." InfluenceWatch, February 27, 2023. https://www.influencewatch.org/non-profit/tides-foundation/.

134. Ibid.

135. "Google Foundation." InfluenceWatch, February 1, 2019. https://www.influencewatch.org/non-profit/google-foundation/.

136. Defund the Police, Home Page, accessed October 4, 2022, www.defundthepolice.org/.

137. Malcolm Gladwell, *Talking to Strangers: What We Should Know About the People We Don't Know* (New York, Little, Brown and Company, September 10, 2019), 306.

138. Ibid., 337.

139. Ibid., 343–344.

140. "Alternatives to Police Services," Defund The Police, September 20, 2020, https://defundthepolice.org/alternatives-to-police-services/.

141. Zusha Elinson, Dan Frosch, and Joshua Jamerson, "Cities Reverse Defunding the Police amid Rising Crime," *WSJ*, May 26, 2021, https://web.archive.org/web/20210813064745/https://www.wsj.com/articles/cities-reverse-defunding-the-police-amid-rising-crime-11622066307.

142. Tim Pool, Timcast, "SF Is Done, Hilton Hotel Surrenders Property as Crime and Violence Drive Away Tourists," YouTube Video, 10:51, June 7, 2023. https://www.youtube.com/watch?v=f1sohK9mCm4.

143. Ari Hoffman, "Seattle fire department reels after 2 attempts to steal fire engines," *The Post Millennial, American News*, June 6 2023, https://thepostmillennial.com/seattle-fire-department-reels-after-2-attempts-to-steal-fire-engines.

144. Ibid.

145. Sofi Sinozich and Lynn Langton, "Rape and Sexual Assault Victimization among College-Age Females, 1995–2013," Bureau of Justice Statistics, US Department of Justice, December 2014, https://bjs.ojp.gov/content/pub/pdf/rsavcaf9513.pdf.

146. Ibid.

147. Ibid.

148. Rob Kuznia, "Once nicknamed 'Murderapolis,' the city that became the center of the 'Defund the Police' movement is grappling with heightened violent crime," CNN, September 25, 2022.

149. Ibid.

150. Ibid.

151. Ibid.

152. Channel 4 News, Cathy Newman and Jordan B Peterson, "Jordan Peterson debate on the gender pay gap, campus protests and post-modernism," YouTube Video, 29:55 January 16, 2018, https://www.youtube.com/watch?v=aMcjxSThD54.

153. Mia Ashton, "California bill aims to make it illegal to criticize teachers for instructing in gender ideology," *The Post Millennial, American News*, April 19, 2023, https://thepostmillennial.com/california-bill-aims-to-make-it-illegal-to-criticize-teachers-for-instructing-in-gender-ideology.

154. University of Chicago Institute of Politics, Van Jones, "CLIP: Van Jones on safe spaces on college campuses," YouTube Video, 4:41, February 24, 2017, https://www.youtube.com/watch?v=Zms3EqGbFOk.

155. Sam Dorman, "Denver elementary school under fire for planning 'families of color playground night,'" FOX News Network, December 15, 2021, https://www.foxnews.com/us/denver-school-playground-families-color.

156. Christopher F. Rufo, "Walmart vs. Whiteness," Christopher F. Rufo, Substack, October 14, 2021, https://christopherrufo.com/walmart-vs-whiteness/.

157. John A. Daly, "Boy Scouts to Accept Girls; Is This Such a Bad Idea?" *Bernard Goldberg's Commentary*, October 17, 2017. https://www.bernardgoldberg.com/p/boy-scouts-to-accept-girls-is-this-such-a-bad-idea.

158. "RIGHTS OF TRANSGENDER AND GENDER-EXPANSIVE STUDENTS POLICY: 8040," 21000 Education Court, Ashburn, VA 20148, Phone: 571-252-1000 BoardDocs® Pro. Loudoun County Public School District, December 3, 2019. https://go.boarddocs.com/vsba/loudoun/Board.nsf/Public.

159. Mark Lungariello, "Virginia teen pleads no contest to second in-school assault," *The New York Post*, November 15, 2021, https://nypost.

com/2021/11/15/virginia-teen-pleads-no-contest-to-second-in-school-assault/.

160. Mark Lungariello, "Virginia board member resigns amid handling of sex assault claims,". *The New York Post*, October 15, 2021, https://web.archive.org/web/20211015232207/https://nypost.com/2021/10/15/virginia-board-member-resigns-amid-handling-of-sex-assault-claim/.

161. Nayan Karel, "WI SPA - Viral video shows a woman complaining about a transgender female being allowed to disrobe," YouTube Video, 3:25, July 13, 2021. https://www.youtube.com/watch?v=2d6Hgu8RT0k.

162. Ibid.

163. Andrew Boryga, "Protests Turn Violent Outside Los Angeles Spa Featured on Tucker Carlson's Show," *The Daily Beast*, July 3, 2021, https://www.thedailybeast.com/protest-turns-violent-outside-wi-spa-los-angeles-over-transgender-customer?ref=home&utm_source=ground.news&utm_medium=referral.

164. Evan Urquhart, "Violence Over an Alleged Transphobic Hoax Shows the Danger of Underestimating Anti-Trans Hate," *Slate*, July 9, 2021, https://slate.com/human-interest/2021/07/wi-spa-la-transphobic-protest.html.

165. Bhavesh Purohit, "When transgender fighter Fallon Fox broke her opponent's skull in MMA fight," *Sportskeeda*, September 30, 2021, https://www.sportskeeda.com/mma/news-when-transgender-fighter-fallon-fox-broke-opponent-s-skull-mma-fight.

166. Tom Cleary, "Athlete Slams Joe Rogan: 'Cancel His Show Already,'" Heavy.com, March 26, 2021, https://heavy.com/news/joe-rogan/fallon-fox-transphobic-comments/.

167. Anne Lepesant, "Penn's Lia Thomas Breaks 200/500 Free Records in Meet with Princeton, Cornell," *SwimSwam*, November 21, 2021, https://swimswam.com/penns-lia-thomas-breaks-200-500-free-records-in-meet-with-princeton-cornell/.

168. Kenneth Garger, "Upenn transgender swimmer continues dominant season with more record-breaking wins," *The New York Post*, December 7, 2021, https://nypost.com/2021/12/07/upenn-transgender-swimmer-lia-thomas-continues-dominant-season-with-more-record-breaking-wins/.

169. Ryan Glasspiegel, "Transgender swimmer Lia Thomas wins women's 500-yard NCAA title," *The New York Post*, March 17, 2022, https://nypost.com/2022/03/17/trans-swimmer-lia-thomas-wins-womens-500-yard-ncaa-title/.

170. Dylan Gwinn, "Trans Cyclists Finish 1st and 2nd, Kiss on Podium Next to 3rd Place Mom Holding Her Baby," Breitbart, June 4, 2022, https://www.breitbart.com/sports/2022/06/04/trans-cyclists-finish-1st-and-2nd-kiss-on-podium-next-to-3rd-place-mom-holding-her-baby/.

171. Ryan Morik, "Transgender female cross-country runner dominating new competition after struggling against boys," FOX News Network, November 17, 2022, https://www.foxnews.com/sports/transgender-female-dominating-new-cross-country-competition-struggling-boys.

172. Matt Lavietes, "'Jeopardy!' champ Amy Schneider Becomes show's top female earner," NBCUniversal News Group, December 28, 2021, https://www.nbcnews.com/nbc-out/out-pop-culture/jeopardy-champ-amy-schneider-becomes-shows-top-female-earner-rcna10180.

173. Dylan Housman, "Transgender Biden Admin Official Named One of USA Today's 'Women of the Year,'" *The Daily Caller*, March 15, 2022, https://dailycaller.com/2022/03/15/rachel-levine-transgender-woman-of-the-year-usa-today/.

174. Jesse O'Neill, "White House dragged for honoring trans woman on International Women's Day," *The New York Post*, March 9, 2023, https://nypost.com/2023/03/09/alba-rueda-trans-woman-honored-by-white-house-on-international-womans-day/.

175. Lydia Hawken and Jaqui Deevoy, "Student, 19, becomes Miss America's first ever transgender local pageant winner as critics accuse the 'woke' competition of 'allowing opportunities to be stolen away from female contestants,'" *The Daily Mail*, Associated Newspapers, November 16, 2022, https://www.dailymail.co.uk/femail/article-11430725/Teen-Miss-Americas-transgender-local-title-holder-critics-blast-woke-competition.html.

176. Azeen Ghorayshi, "Report Reveals Sharp Rise in Transgender Young People in the U.S.," *The New York Times*, June 10, 2022, https://web.archive.org/web/20230114051216/https://www.

nytimes.com/2022/06/10/science/transgender-teenagers-national-survey.html.

177. "Data on Transgender Youth," The Trevor Project, February 22, 2019, https://www.thetrevorproject.org/research-briefs/data-on-transgender-youth/.

178. Spector, Harlan. "Akron Children's Helps Transgender Ryace Boyer Be Her True Self." Inside Children's Blog, December 30, 2021. https://web.archive.org/web/20220124171703/https://www.akronchildrens.org/inside/2021/06/07/akron-childrens-helps-transgender-ryace-boyer-be-her-true-self/.

179. "Puberty Blockers," St. Louis Children's Hospital, 2020, https://www.stlouischildrens.org/conditions-treatments/transgender-center/puberty-blockers.

180. Ibid.

181. "Puberty Blockers," Patient and Family Education, Adolescent Medicine, Seattle Children's Hospital, December 2019, https://www.seattlechildrens.org/pdf/PE2572.pdf.

182. Ibid.

183. Justine Schober, M.D., "Lupron Sex Offender Therapy - Full Text View," ClinicalTrials.gov, September 22, 2005, https://clinicaltrials.gov/ct2/show/NCT00220350.

184. Fan Liang, M.D., "Top Surgery (Chest Feminization or Chest Masculinization)," Johns Hopkins Medicine, January 19, 2023, https://www.hopkinsmedicine.org/health/treatment-tests-and-therapies/top-surgery.

185. Ibid.

186. "Phalloplasty," Boston Children's Hospital, 2022, https://www.childrenshospital.org/treatments/phalloplasty.

187. "Vaginoplasty," Boston Children's Hospital, accessed through Wayback Machine, August 2, 2022, https://web.archive.org/web/20220802022337/https://www.childrenshospital.org/treatments/vaginoplasty.

188. Curtis Crane, M.D., "Phalloplasty and metoidioplasty - overview and postoperative considerations," Gender Affirming Health Program,

University of California, San Francisco, June 17, 2016, https://transcare.ucsf.edu/guidelines/phalloplasty.

189. Christina Buttons, "REVEALED: leading trans health group recommends lowering ages for medical gender transition," *The Post Millennial*, September 11, 2022, https://thepostmillennial.com/revealed-leading-trans-health-group-recommends-lowering-ages-for-medical-gender-transition.

190. "Vaginoplasty," Boston Children's Hospital, 2022, https://www.childrenshospital.org/treatments/vaginoplasty.

191. "WPATH-Connected Transgender 'Health' Doctors Prescribe Puberty Blockers to Minors as Young as Eight Years Old and Irreversible 'Cross-Gender Hormones' to Minors as Young as 14 Years Old ... 'Most Kids Are Mature Enough to Make a Relatively Informed Decision,'" Project Veritas, April 19, 2023 https://www.projectveritas.com/news/wpath-connected-transgender-health-doctors-prescribe-puberty-blockers-to/.

192. Project Veritas, "CA High School Teacher Admits Communist Indoctrination of Students: 'Turn Them into Revolutionaries,'" YouTube Video, 12:06, August 31, 2021, https://www.youtube.com/watch?v=83b_u5V51U8&t=1s.

193. Andrew Mark Miller, "Denver public school teaching kindergartners BLM 'guiding principles' including disruption of nuclear family,'" FOX News Network, January 21, 2022, https://www.foxnews.com/politics/denver-public-school-teaching-kindergartners-blm-guiding-principles-including-disruption-nuclear-family.

194. "Elite Chicago Private School's Dean of Students Brags About Bringing in LGBTQ+ Health Center to Teach 'Queer Sex' to Minors ... 'That's a Really Cool Part of My Job' ... 'Passing Around Dildos and Butt Plugs' ... 'Using Lube Versus Using Spit,'" Project Veritas, December 7, 2022, https://www.projectveritas.com/news/elite-chicago-private-schools-dean-of-students-brags-about-bringing-in-lgbtq/.

195. Greg Wilson, "Dallas Gay Bar's Drag Show for Kids, Obscene Sign Draws Angry Protests," *The Daily Wire*, June 5, 2022. https://www.dailywire.com/news/dallas-gay-bars-drag-show-for-kids-obscene-sign-draws-angry-protests.

196. Brody Levesque, "'Stop Grooming the Kids,' right-wing protests Dallas Drag event at gay bar," *Los Angeles Blade,* June 5, 2022, https://www.losangelesblade.com/2022/06/05/stop-grooming-the-kids-right-wingers-protest-dallas-drag-event-at-gay-bar/.

197. Harper Keenan and Lil Miss Hot Mess, "Drag pedagogy: The playful practice of queer imagination in early childhood," *Curriculum Inquiry,* vol. 50, no. 5 (2020), https://doi.org/10.1080/03626784.2020.186 4621, 440–61.

198. "SB 5599 - 2023-24: Supporting youth and young adults seeking protected health care services," Washington State Legislature, April 15, 2023, https://app.leg.wa.gov/billsummary?BillNumber=5599&-Year=2023&Initiative=false.

199. "Declaration of Independence: A Transcript," National Archives, accessed November 15, 2022, www.archives.gov/founding-docs/declaration-transcript.

200. "Abraham Lincoln Letter to Joshua Speed," August 24, 1855, Abraham Lincoln Online, accessed November 15, 2022, www.abrahamlincolnonline.org/lincoln/speeches/speed.htm.

201. "Plessy v. Ferguson," National Archives, accessed November 15, 2022, www.archives.gov/milestone-documents/plessy-v-ferguson.

202. Ibid.

203. "Separate is Not Equal, Brown v. Board of Education," Smithsonian *National Museum of American History,* accessed November 15, 2022, www.americanhistory.si.edu/brown/history/1-segregated/detail/jim-crow-laws.html.

204. Ibid.

205. "1921 Tulsa Race Massacre," Tulsa Historical Society and Museum, accessed November 15, 2022, www.tulsahistory.org/exhibit/1921-tulsa-race-massacre/.

206. "The Tale of Two Wolves," Naticoke Indian Tribe, accessed November 15, 2022, www.nanticokeindians.org/page/tale-of-two-wolves.

207. James Truslow Adams, "Quotable Quotes," GoodReads, accessed November 16, 2022, www.goodreads.com/quotes/235517-the-american-dream-is-that-dream-of-a-land-in.

208. Emma Lazarus, "The New Colossus," Poetry Foundation, accessed November 16, 2022, www.poetryfoundation.org/poems/46550/the-new-colossus.

209. Abby Budiman, "Key findings about U.S. immigrants," Pew Research Center, August 20, 2020, www.pewresearch.org/fact-tank/2020/08/20/key-findings-about-u-s-immigrants/.

210. "The Immigration Act of 1924 (The Johnson-Reed Act)," U.S. Department of State, Office of the Historian, accessed November 16, 2022, www.history.state.gov/milestones/1921-1936/immigration-act/.

211. Abby Budiman, "Key findings about U.S. immigrants," Pew Research Center, August 20, 2020, www.pewresearch.org/fact-tank/2020/08/20/key-findings-about-u-s-immigrants/.

212. Ibid.

213. Jeanne Batalova et al., "Frequently Requested Statistics on Immigrants and Immigration in the United States," Migration Policy Institute, February 11, 2021, www.migrationpolicy.org/article/frequently-requested-statistics-immigrants-and-immigration-united-states-2020.

214. Ibid.

215. Matthew Zane, "What Percentage of the Workforce is Female?" Zippia.com, March 1, 2022, www.zippia.com/advice/what-percentage-of-the-workforce-is-female/.

216. Niti Samani, "Differences Between a part-Time and Full-Time Employee," Deskera, accessed November 17, 2022, www.deskera.com/blog/parttime-fulltime-employee/.

217. Markham Heid, "Why Do Women Live Longer Than Men?" TIME, February 27, 2019, time.com/5538099/why-do-women-live-longer-than-men/.

218. Daniel A. Cox, "Men's Social Circles are Shrinking," Survey Center on American Life, June 29, 2021, www.americansurveycenter.org/why-mens-social-circles-are-shrinking/.

219. Channel 4 News, "Jordan Peterson debate on the gender pay gap, campus protests, and postmodernism," YouTube Video, 29:55, January 16, 2018, www.youtube.com/watch?v=aMcjxSThD54.

220. Locke, John. The Two Treatises of Civil Government (Hollis ed.). London: A. Millar et al., 1689. https://oll.libertyfund.org/title/hollis-the-two-treatises-of-civil-government-hollis-ed.

221. "John Locke and the Natural Law Tradition," Natural Law, Natural Rights and American Constitutionalism, accessed November 17, 2022, www.nlnrac.org/earlymodern/locke#

222. "The Bill of Rights: A Transcription," National Archives, accessed November 17, 2022, www.archives.gov/founding-docs/bill-of-rights-transcript.

223. George Orwell, "Quotable Quotes," GoodReads, accessed November 17, 2022, www.goodreads.com/quotes/342655-the-great-enemy-of-clear-language-is-insincerity-when-there.

224. Vladimir Lenin, BrainyQuote, accessed November 17, 2022, www.brainyquote.com/quotes/vladimir_lenin_383393.

225. Jonathan Butcher and Mike Gonzalez, "Critical Race Theory, the New Intolerance, and Its Grip on America," The Heritage Foundation, December 7, 2020, www.heritage.org/sites/default/files/2020-12/BG3567.pdf.

226. Cornel West, *Critical Race Theory: The Key Writings That Formed the Movement*, Foreword, edited by Kimberlé Crenshaw, Neil Gotanda, Gary Peller, and Kendall Thomas, (New York, NY: The New press, 2010), xiii-xiii.

227. Gregg Sangillo, "Antiracism in Action: Ibram Kendi Offers Hard Truths and Real Solutions," American University, Washington D.C., August 20, 2019, www.american.edu/ucm/news/20190820-kendi-antiracism.cfm.

228. Michael Harriot, The Root, "Unpacking the Attacks on Critical Race Theory," YouTube Video, 45:27, September 21, 2021, https://www.youtube.com/watch?v=efjZqmVKm9Q.

229. Derek A. Bell, Jr., "Serving Two Masters: Integration Ideals and Client Interests in School Desegregation Litigation," Yale Law Journal , vol. 85, no.4, 470-516 (March 1976), www.law.nyu.edu/sites/default/files/Serving%20Two%20Masters.pdf.

230. Derek A. Bell, Jr., "Brown v. Board of Education and the Interest Convergence Dilemma," *Harvard Law Review*, vol. 93, no. 3, 518-533,

(January 1980), www.jstor.org/stable/1340546#metadata_info_tab_contents.

231. Jelani Cobb, "The Man Behind Critical Race Theory," *The New Yorker*, September 20, 2021, www.newyorker.com/magazine/2021/09/20/the-man-behind-critical-race-theory.

232. Kimberlee Crenshaw, "Demarginalizing the Intersection of Race and Sex: A Black Feminist Critique of Antidiscrimination Doctrine, Feminist Theory, and Antiracist Politics," *University of Chicago Legal Forum*, vol. 189, article 8, www.chicagounbound.uchicago.edu/cgi/viewcontent.cgi?article=1052&context=uclf.

233. Kimberlee Creshawn, "Why intersectionality can't wait," *The Washington Post*, September 24, 2015, www.washingtonpost.com/news/in-theory/wp/2015/09/24/why-intersectionality-cant-wait/.

234. "Bio" Ibram X. Kendi website, accessed November 20, 2022, www.ibramxkendi.com/bio.

235. Ibram X. Kendi, *How to Be an Antiracist* (New York, NY: One World, 2019), 25–26.

236. Ibid., 20–21.

237. Ibid., 188–89.

238. John Blake, "What's wrong with too many white men in one place?" CNN, May 27, 2017, www.cnn.com/2017/05/25/us/too-many-white-men.

239. "Read Martin Luther King Jr.'s 'I Have a Dream' speech in its entirety," NPR – KQED, January 14, 2022, www.npr.org/2010/01/18/122701268/i-have-a-dream-speech-in-its-entirety.

240. Corinne Bendersky, "Making U.S. Fire Departments More Diverse and Inclusive," *Harvard Business Review*, December 7, 2018, www.hbr.org/2018/12/making-u-s-fire-departments-more-diverse-and-inclusive.

241. "Executive Order 13583-- Establishing a Coordinated Government-Wide Initiative to Promote Diversity and Inclusion in the Federal Workforce." National Archives and Records Administration, August 18, 2011. https://obamawhitehouse.archives.gov/the-press-office/2011/08/18/executive-order-13583-establishing-coordinated-government-wide-initiativ.

242. "FACT SHEET: 100 Days in Biden-Harris Administration Makes History with Presidential Appointees," The White House, April 29, 2021, www.whitehouse.gov/briefing-room/statements-releases/2021/04/29/fact-sheet-100-days-in-biden-harris-administration-makes-history-with-presidential-appointees/.

243. Kate Conger, "Exclusive: Here's the Full 10-Page Anti-diversity Screed Circulating Internally at Google," Gizmodo, August 5, 2017, www.gizmodo.com/exclusive-heres-the-full-10-page-anti-diversity-screed-1797564320.

244. Ibid.

245. Mark Bergen and Ellen Huet, "Google Fires Author of Divisive Memo on Gender Differences," Bloomberg, August 8, 2017, https://web.archive.org/web/20170812202025/https://www.bloomberg.com/news/articles/2017-08-08/google-fires-employee-behind-controversial-diversity-memo.

246. Charlie Nash, "Apple Diversity VP: Diversity is More than Focusing on 'Race, Gender, and Sexual Orientation,'" Breitbart, October 12, 2017, www.breitbart.com/tech/2017/10/12/apple-diversity-vp-diversity-is-more-than-focusing-on-race-gender-and-sexual-orientation/.

247. Gabe Kaminsky, "EXCLUSIVE: Public University UVA Spent Nearly $541 per Minute for Ibram Kendi 'Racial Equity' Lecture," The Daily Wire, February 9, 2022,https://www.dailywire.com/news/exclusive-uva-a-public-university-spent-nearly-541-per-minute-for-ibram-kendi-racial-equity-lecture.

248. Chrissy Clark, "Analysis: Ibram X. Kendi Raked in Over $300,000 in Speaking Fees," The Daily Wire, March 16, 2021, www.dailywire.com/news/analysis-ibram-x-kendi-raked-in-over-300000-in-speaking-fees.

249. Ibram X. Kendi, "Ibram X. Kendi defines what it means to be an antiracist," Penguin UK, June 9, 2020, www.penguin.co.uk/articles/2020/06/ibram-x-kendi-definition-of-antiracist.

250. Dylan Matthews, "The case against equality of opportunity," Vox, September 21, 2015, www.vox.com/2015/9/21/9334215/equality-of-opportunity/.

251. "Executive Order 13985 – Advancing Racial Equity and Support for Underserved Communities Throughout the Federal Government,"

American Presidency Project, UC Santa Barbara, January 20, 2021, www.presidency.ucsb.edu/documents/executive-order-13985-advancing-racial-equity-and-support-for-underserved-communities/.

252. "Executive Order 8802: Prohibition of Discrimination in the Defense Industry," National Archives, (1941), www.archives.gov/milestone-documents/executive-order-8802.

253. "Executive Order 9981: Desegregation of the Armed Forces," National Archives, (1948), www.archives.gov/milestone-documents/executive-order-9981.

254. Kaelan Deese, "Oregon governor signs bill ending reading and math proficiency requirements for graduation," Yahoo News, August 10, 2021, www.news.yahoo.com/oregon-governor-signs-bill-ending-154100667.html/.

255. Hillary Burrud, "Gov. Kate Brown signed a law to allow Oregon students to graduate without proving they can write or do math. She doesn't want to talk about it," *The Oregonian*, August 13, 2021, www.oregonlive.com/politics/2021/08/gov-kate-brown-signed-a-law-to-allow-oregon-students-to-graduate-without-proving-they-can-write-or-do-math-she-doesnt-want-to-talk-about-it.html.

256. Rachel Alexander, Salem Reporter. "Vote 2022: Oregon's next Governor Will Shape Education for a Generation of Students." Oregon Capital Chronicle, October 19, 2022. https://oregoncapital chronicle.com/2022/10/17/oregons-next-governor-will-shape-education-of-a-generation-of-students/.

257. "Washington HB 1692 – Promoting Racial Equity in the Criminal Legal System by Eliminating Drive-By Shooting as a Basis for Elevating Murder in the First Degree to Aggravated Murder in the First Degree," Track-Bill, December 23, 2021, www.trackbill.com/bill/washington-house-bill-1692-promoting-racial-equity-in-the-criminal-legal-system-by-eliminating-drive-by-shooting-as-a-basis-for-elevating-murder-in-the-first-degree-to-aggravated-murder-in-the-first-degree/2174130/.

258. "California Proposition 16, Repeal Proposition 209, Affirmative Action Amendment (2020)," Ballotopedia, accessed November 20,

2022, www.ballotpedia.org/California_Proposition_16,_Repeal_Proposition_209_Affirmative_Action_Amendment_(2020).

259. "California Proposition 209, Affirmative Action Initiative (1996)," Ballotopedia, accessed November 20, 2022, www.ballotpedia.org/California_Proposition_209,_Affirmative_Action_Initiative_(1996).

260. Ibid.

261. Ibid.

262. "American Rescue Plan," The White House, accessed November 20, 2022, www.whitehouse.gov/american-rescue-plan/.

263. "FY 2022 Harm Reduction Program Grant," Substance Abuse and Mental Health Services Administration, U.S. Department of Health and Human Services, January 25, 2022, https://www.samhsa.gov/sites/default/files/grants/pdf/fy22-harm-reduction-nofo.pdf.

264. "Executive Order 13985 – Advancing Racial Equity and Support for Underserved Communities Throughout the Federal Government," The American Presidency Project, UC Santa Barbara, January 20, 2021, www.presidency.ucsb.edu/documents/executive-order-13985-advancing-racial-equity-and-support-for-underserved-communities/.

265. Patrick Hauf, "Yes, Safe Smoking Kits Include Free Crack Pipes. We Know Because We Got Them," *The Washington Free Beacon*, May 12, 2022, www.freebeacon.com/biden-administration/yes-safe-smoking-kits-include-free-crack-pipes-we-know-because-we-got-them/.

266. Michael Shellenberger on Twitter, "1. TWITTER FILES, PART 4, The Removal of Donald Trump: January 7, As the pressure builds, Twitter executives build the case for a permanent ban" (@shellenberger, December 10, 2022), https://twitter.com/shellenberger/status/1601720455005511680.

267. David Lammy and Manish Bapna, "There Is No Climate Justice without Racial Justice," *TIME*, May 3, 2021, https://time.com/6017907/climate-emergency-racial-justice/.

268. Bari Weiss on Twitter, "THREAD: THE TWITTER FILES PART TWO. TWITTER'S SECRET BLACKLISTS," (@bariweiss, December 8, 2022), https://twitter.com/bariweiss/status/1601007575633305600.

269. Timcast IRL, "Timcast IRL - Anheuser Busch Market Cap Drops Billions as Boycott Worsens w/Peter Boghossian." YouTube Video, 2:03:55,

April 10, 2023. https://www.youtube.com/watch?v=r9kJ0LeECxA& list=PLErukX1W1OYjFx2pG8zjWiMuPMG0F-LbI&index=6.

270. Matt Taibbi on Twitter, "1. THREAD: The Twitter Files, Part Six, TWITTER, THE FBI SUBSIDIARY," (@mtaibbi, December 16, 2022), https://twitter.com/mtaibbi/status/1603857534737072128.

271. Martin Luther King, Jr., "Letter from a Birmingham Jail" (New York, Harper Collins Publishers, 1963, 1994), 1.

272. Ibid., 3–4.

273. Ibid., 22–23.

274. "[Video] Leaked Insider Recording from ABC News Reveals Network Executives Killed Bombshell Story Implicating Jeffrey Epstein," Project Veritas, November 19, 2019, https://www.projectveritas.com/news/ video-leaked-insider-recording-from-abc-news-reveals-network- executives-killed-bombshell-story-implicating-jeffrey-epstein/.

275. George Orwell, *1984* (Penguin Books, 1990), https://www.orwell.ru/ library/novels/1984/english/en_app.

276. The Podcast of the Lotus Eaters, "What Is Wokeism?" YouTube Video, 20:41, March 16, 2023. https://www.youtube.com/watch? v=P3_aQyXTv-Q.

ABOUT THE AUTHORS

David Johnson is an engineer born and raised in upstate New York during the late '90s. Growing up in an area where it was not uncommon to see families of all cultural backgrounds, he grew up experiencing "diversity" in its most accurate form, where ethnicity was never the defining feature of anyone in his social group. And while the aesthetics and cuisine of each family home might have differed, shared values of a hard work ethic and a respect for the values of America were constant.

After graduating from the Rochester Institute of Technology and working in Portland, Oregon for a few years, David Johnson was able to witness the end result of progressive ideology in one of the most Leftist places in the country.

Kent Heckenlively is an attorney, science teacher, and *New York Times* bestselling author of more than a dozen books. His books have sold more than a quarter of a million copies and have been translated into several languages. His book *Plague of Corruption* is being turned into a documentary film narrated by Liam Neeson.

Made in the USA
Las Vegas, NV
29 November 2023

81809473R00125